HBR's 10 Must Reads

UPDATED & EXPANDED

I0109782

Decision Making

HBR's 10 Must Reads

HBR's 10 Must Reads are definitive collections of classic ideas, practical advice, and essential thinking from the pages of *Harvard Business Review*. Exploring topics like disruptive innovation, emotional intelligence, and new technology in our ever-evolving world, these books empower any leader to make bold decisions and inspire others.

TITLES INCLUDE:

> HBR's 10 Must Reads for New Managers
> HBR's 10 Must Reads on Artificial Intelligence
> HBR's 10 Must Reads on Building a Great Culture
> HBR's 10 Must Reads on Change Management
> HBR's 10 Must Reads on Communication
> HBR's 10 Must Reads on Data Strategy
> HBR's 10 Must Reads on Decision-Making
> HBR's 10 Must Reads on Emotional Intelligence
> HBR's 10 Must Reads on High Performance
> HBR's 10 Must Reads on Innovation
> HBR's 10 Must Reads on Leadership
> HBR's 10 Must Reads on Leading Digital Transformation
> HBR's 10 Must Reads on Leading Winning Teams
> HBR's 10 Must Reads on Managing People
> HBR's 10 Must Reads on Managing Yourself
> HBR's 10 Must Reads on Marketing
> HBR's 10 Must Reads on Mental Toughness
> HBR's 10 Must Reads on Strategy
> HBR's 10 Must Reads on Women and Leadership
> HBR's 10 Must Reads Boxed Set (6 books)
> HBR's 10 Must Reads Ultimate Boxed Set (14 books)

For a full list, visit hbr.org/mustreads.

HBR's 10 Must Reads

UPDATED & EXPANDED

Decision Making

Harvard Business Review Press
Boston, Massachusetts

Copyright 2026 Harvard Business Publishing Corporation

All rights reserved

Printed in the United States of America

10 9 8 7 6 5 4 3 2 1

No part of this publication may be reproduced, stored in or introduced into a retrieval system, or transmitted, in any form, or by any means (electronic, mechanical, photocopying, recording, or otherwise), without the prior permission of the publisher. Requests for permission should be directed to permissions@harvardbusiness.org, or mailed to Permissions, Harvard Business School Publishing, 60 Harvard Way, Boston, Massachusetts 02163.

The web addresses referenced in this book were live and correct at the time of the book's publication but may be subject to change.

Cataloging-in-Publication data is forthcoming.

ISBN: 979-8-89279-300-1
eISBN: 979-8-89279-301-8

The paper used in this publication meets the requirements of the American National Standard for Permanence of Paper for Publications and Documents in Libraries and Archives Z39.48-1992.

Contents

HBR's 10 Must Reads

UPDATED & EXPANDED

_____

Decision Making

1

How to Tackle Your Toughest Decisions

by Joseph L. Badaracco

Every manager makes tough calls—it comes with the job. And the toughest calls come in the gray areas—situations where you and your team have worked hard to gather the facts and done the best analysis you can, but you still don't know what to do. It's easy to become paralyzed in the face of such challenges. Yet as a leader, you have to make a decision and move forward. Your judgment becomes critical.

Judgment is hard to define. It is a fusion of your thinking, feelings, experience, imagination, and character. But five practical questions can improve your odds of making sound judgments, even when the data is incomplete or unclear, opinions are divided, and the answers are far from obvious.

Where do these questions come from? Over many centuries and across many cultures, they have emerged as men and women with serious responsibilities have struggled with difficult problems. They express the insights of the most penetrating minds and compassionate spirits of human history. I have relied on them for years, in teaching MBA candidates and counseling executives, and I believe that they can help you, your team, and your organization navigate the grayest of gray areas.

This article explains the five questions and illustrates them with a disguised case study involving a manager who must decide what to do about a persistently underperforming employee who has failed to respond to suggestions for improvement. He deserves a bad review, if not dismissal, but higher-ups at the company want to overlook his failings.

How should the manager approach this situation? Not by following her gut instinct. Not by simply falling into line. Instead, she needs to systematically work through the five questions:

What are the net, net consequences of all my options?

What are my core obligations?

What will work in the world as it is?

Who are we?

What can I live with?

To grapple with these questions, you must rely on the best information and expertise available. But in the end you have to answer them for yourself. With gray-area decisions, you can never be certain you've made the right call. But if you follow this process, you'll know that you worked on the problem in the right way—not just as a good manager but as a thoughtful human being.

Net, Net Consequences

The first question asks you to thoroughly and analytically consider every course of action available to you, along with the full,

Idea in Brief

The toughest calls managers have to make come in situations when they have worked hard to gather the facts and have done the best analysis they can, but they still don't know what to do. Then judgment—a fusion of thinking, feelings, experience, imagination, and character—becomes critical. Five practical questions can improve your odds of making sound judgments:

- What are the net, net consequences of all my options?
- What are my core obligations?
- What will work in the world as it is?
- Who are we?
- What can I live with?

With gray-area decisions, you can never be certain that you've made the right call. But if you work through these questions, you'll know that you've approached the problem in the right way—not just as a good manager but as a thoughtful human being.

real-world, human consequences of each. Gray-area problems are rarely resolved in a flash of intuitive brilliance from one person; as a very successful CEO told me, "The lonely leader on Olympus is really a bad model." So your job is to put aside your initial assumption about what you *should* do, gather a group of trusted advisers and experts, and ask yourself and them, "What *could* we do? And who will be hurt or helped, short-term and long-term, by each option?"

Don't confuse this with cost-benefit analysis, or focus solely on what you can count or price. Of course, you should get the best data you can and apply the relevant frameworks. But gray-area problems require you to think more broadly, deeply, concretely, imaginatively, and objectively about the full impact of your choices. In the words of the ancient Chinese philosopher Mozi, "It is the business of the benevolent man to seek to promote what is beneficial to the world and to eliminate what is harmful."

In today's complex, fluid, interdependent world, none of us can predict the future with total accuracy. And it's sometimes hard to think clearly about gray-area issues. What's important is taking the time to open your mind, assemble the right team, and analyze your options through a humanist lens. You might sketch out a rough decision tree, listing all potential moves and all probable outcomes, or designate certain people to act as devil's advocates to find holes in your thinking and prevent you from rushing to conclusions or succumbing to groupthink.

When you make important, difficult decisions, you affect many people's lives and livelihoods. The first question asks you to grapple hard with that reality.

Core Obligations

We all have duties—as parents, children, citizens, employees. Managers also have duties to shareholders and other stakeholders. But the second question gets at something deeper: the duties we have to safeguard and respect the lives, rights, and dignity of our fellow men and women.

All the world's great religions—Islam, Judaism, Hinduism, Christianity—emphasize this obligation. The contemporary ethicist Kwame Anthony Appiah has said, "No local loyalty can ever justify forgetting that each human being has responsibilities to every other."

How can you figure out specifically what these duties oblige you to do in a particular situation? By relying on what philosophers call your "moral imagination." That involves stepping out of your comfort zone, recognizing your biases and blind spots, and putting yourself in the shoes of all key stakeholders, especially the most vulnerable ones. How would you feel in their place? What would you be most concerned about or afraid of? How would you want to be treated? What would you see as fair? What rights would you believe you had? What would you consider to be hateful? You might speak directly to the people who will be affected by your decision, or ask a member of your team to role-play the outsider or victim as persuasively as they can.

Again, you must look past economics and your business school training. Yes, managers have a legal duty to serve the corporation—but that's a very broad mandate that includes the well-being of workers, customers, and the community in which they operate. You have serious obligations to everyone simply because you are a human being. When you face a gray-area decision, you have to think—long, hard, and personally—about which of these duties stands at the head of the line.

The World as It Is

The third question pushes you to look at your problem in a clear-eyed, pragmatic way—seeing the world not as you would like it to be but as it is. Ultimately you need a plan that will work—one that will move an individual, a team, a department, or an entire organization through a gray area responsibly and successfully.

The phrase "the world as it is" points toward Niccolò Machiavelli's thinking—a perspective that might seem surprising in an article about making responsible decisions. But his view is important, because it acknowledges that we don't live in a predictable, calm environment populated with virtuous people. The world Machiavelli described is unpredictable, difficult, and shaped by self-interest. Sound plans can turn out badly, and bad plans sometimes work. Much of what happens is simply beyond our control. Leaders rarely have unlimited freedom and resources, so they must often make painful choices. And a great many individuals and groups will pursue their own agendas, skillfully or clumsily, if not persuaded to do otherwise.

That is why, after considering consequences and duties, you need to think about practicalities: Of the possible solutions to your problem, which is most likely to work? Which is most resilient? And how resilient and flexible are you?

To answer those questions, you need to map the force field of power around you: who wants what and how hard and successfully each person can fight for his aims. You must also ready yourself to be agile and even opportunistic—maneuvering around any roadblocks or surprises—and, when the situation calls for it, to play hardball, asserting your authority and reminding others who is the boss.

It's easy to misinterpret the third question as an "out"—an excuse to do what's safe and expedient instead of the right thing. But the question is really about what will work if you bring persistence, dedication, creativity, prudent risk-taking, and political savvy to the task.

Who Are We?

According to an old African adage, "I am because we are." Put differently, our behavior and identities are shaped by the groups in which we work and live. As Aristotle said (and as a vast body of scientific literature has since confirmed), "Man is by nature a social animal." So this question asks you to step back and think about your decision in terms of relationships, values, and norms.

What really matters to your team, company, community, culture? How can you act in a way that reflects and expresses those belief systems? If they conflict, which should take precedence? To answer those questions, you might think about the defining stories of a particular group—the decisions and incidents that everyone cites when explaining the ideals to which you are collectively committed, what you have struggled to achieve, and what outcomes you try hard to avoid. Imagine that you are writing a sentence or a chapter in your company's history. Of all the paths you might choose in this gray area, which would best express what your organization stands for?

This question comes fourth because you shouldn't start with it. Unlike the first three, which require you to take an outsider's perspective on your situation and consider it as objectively as possible, this one addresses you as an insider, at risk for adopting an insular, limited view when you consider norms and values, because we are naturally inclined to take care of our own. So counterbalance that tendency with the thinking prompted by the previous questions.

Living with Your Decision

Good judgment relies on two things: One is the best possible understanding and analysis of the situation. The other involves the values, ideals, vulnerabilities, and experiences of whoever will be making the decision. A seasoned executive once told me, "I wouldn't go ahead with something just because my brain told me it was the right thing to do. I also had to feel it. If I didn't, I had to get my brain and my gut into harmony."

Ultimately you must choose, commit to, act on, and live with the consequences of your choice. So it must also reflect what you really care about as a manager and a human being. After considering outcomes, duties, practicalities, and values, you must decide what matters most and what matters less. This has always been the challenge of taking on any serious responsibilities at work and in life.

How will you figure out what you can live with? End your conversations with others, close the door, mute the electronics, and stop to reflect. Imagine yourself explaining your decision to a close friend or a mentor—someone you trust and respect deeply. Would you feel comfortable? How would that person react? It may also be helpful to write down your decision and your reasons for it: Writing forces clearer thinking and serves as a form of personal commitment.

In Practice

Now let's turn to our case study. Becky Friedman was the 27-year-old manager of a 14-person technology group responsible for clothing sales at an online retailer. One of her team members, Terry Fletcher, a man 15 years her senior with a longer tenure at the company, wasn't doing his part. Although his previous boss had routinely given him scores of 3.5 on their five-point performance scale, Friedman didn't believe his work merited that; and whenever she presented him with opportunities to develop his skills and ramp up his contributions, he failed to follow through. So she wanted to drop his rating to 2.5 and put him on a performance improvement plan (PIP), on a path to dismissal. Soon, however, two of the company's vice presidents, good friends of Fletcher's, caught wind of her plans and paid her a visit. They asked whether she was sure about what she was doing and suggested that the real problem might be her management.

Suddenly the situation was no longer black-and-white. Friedman had entered a gray area and felt stuck. To find a way out, she turned to the five questions. She considered her options—stick to her plan, abandon it, or find a middle ground—and their consequences. She reminded herself of her basic duties to her fellow human beings, including Fletcher, her team, and the VPs. She evaluated the practical realities of her organization. She weighed the defining norms and values of her various social groups. And she thought carefully about her own abiding sense of what really matters in life.

She suspected that if she pushed forward and gave Fletcher the rating he deserved, she and her team would suffer retribution: The VPs could withhold resources or even force her out of the company. She also worried about Fletcher, who seemed off-balance and appeared to have few things going well in his life. How would a poor review and a possible job loss affect him, not just financially but also psychologically? If Friedman chose option B, however, she would still have a deadweight on her team, which might prevent the group from achieving its ambitious goals and demoralize its most talented and diligent members. The VPs might also take her capitulation as a sign of weakness, which could keep her, a relative newcomer, from moving up in the leadership ranks.

Middle-ground options, such as presenting Fletcher with further development opportunities or giving him another warning, seemed more promising but carried their own risks: Would they be effective in changing his behavior? Would they still result in backlash from the VPs? Friedman also thought about what she, her team, and her organization cared about most. As a woman in computer science, she knew what it was like to be marginalized, as Fletcher was among the whiz kids in her department, and she felt compelled to help him. At the same time, her group prided itself on exceptionally professional performance, and her company, although young, had always claimed and generally proved to be a meritocracy with high standards and a sharp focus on customer needs.

After much deliberation, Friedman decided to try a counseling session with Fletcher. She opened by telling him that she had decided to give him a 2.5, but that she wouldn't put him on a PIP because it would be too demeaning. She then asked him to consider the department's recent hires—all of whom had strong technical skills—and honestly evaluate whether he would be happy or successful working alongside them. She concluded by suggesting that he spend the next several months continuing to do his job while also looking for another one. She was surprised and relieved when his immediate anger over the bad rating subsided and he agreed to consider her plan; in fact, he had already been toying with the idea of leaving. He spent the next several weeks looking for other positions, inside the company and elsewhere, and soon joined another company. Friedman, meanwhile, continued to thrive. She had, of course, been lucky; there was no guarantee that Fletcher would respond so positively to her feedback. But she'd put herself in a good position by getting the process right, and she'd been prepared to try other, equally thought-through tactics if the first didn't work.

. . .

When you face a gray-area problem, be sure to systematically answer *all five* of the questions, just as Becky Friedman did. Don't simply pick your favorite. Each question is an important voice in the centuries-long conversation about what counts as a sound decision regarding a hard problem with high stakes for other people.

Leadership can be a heavy burden. It is also a compelling, crucial challenge. In gray areas, your job isn't *finding* solutions; it's *creating* them, relying on your judgment. As an executive I greatly respect once told me, "We really want someone or some rule to tell us what to do. But sometimes there isn't one, and *you* have to decide what the most relevant rules or principles are in this particular case. You can't escape that responsibility."

Originally published in September 2016. Reprint R1609J

2

The Hidden Traps in Decision Making

by John S. Hammond, Ralph L. Keeney, and Howard Raiffa

Making decisions is the most important job of any executive. It's also the toughest and the riskiest. Bad decisions can damage a business and a career, sometimes irreparably. So where do bad decisions come from? In many cases, they can be traced back to the way the decisions were made—the alternatives were not clearly defined, the right information was not collected, the costs and benefits were not accurately weighed. But sometimes the fault lies not in the decision-making process but rather in the mind of the decision maker. The way the human brain works can sabotage our decisions.

Researchers have been studying the way our minds function in making decisions for half a century. This research, in the laboratory and in the field, has revealed that we use unconscious routines to cope with the complexity inherent in most decisions. These routines, known as *heuristics*, serve us well in most situations. In judging distance, for example, our minds frequently rely on a heuristic that equates clarity with proximity. The clearer an object appears, the closer we judge it to be. The fuzzier it appears, the farther away we assume it must be. This simple mental shortcut helps us to make the continuous stream of distance judgments required to navigate the world.

Yet, like most heuristics, it is not foolproof. On days that are hazier than normal, our eyes will tend to trick our minds into thinking that things are more distant than they actually are. Because the resulting distortion poses few dangers for most of us, we can safely ignore it. For airline pilots, though, the distortion can be catastrophic. That's why pilots are trained to use objective measures of distance in addition to their vision.

Researchers have identified a whole series of such flaws in the way we think in making decisions. Some, like the heuristic for clarity, are sensory misperceptions. Others take the form of biases. Others appear simply as irrational anomalies in our thinking. What makes all these traps so dangerous is their invisibility. Because they are hardwired into our thinking process, we fail to recognize them—even as we fall right into them.

For executives, whose success hinges on the many day-to-day decisions they make or approve, the psychological traps are especially dangerous. They can undermine everything from new-product development to acquisition and divestiture strategy to succession planning. While no one can rid his or her mind of these ingrained flaws, anyone can follow the lead of airline pilots and learn to understand the traps and compensate for them.

Idea in Brief

Bad decisions can often be traced back to the way the decisions were made—the alternatives were not clearly defined, the right information was not collected, the costs and benefits were not accurately weighed. But sometimes the fault lies not in the decision-making process but rather in the mind of the decision maker: The way the human brain works can sabotage the choices we make. In this article, first published in 1998, John S. Hammond, Ralph L. Keeney, and Howard Raiffa examine eight psychological traps that can affect the way we make business decisions. The anchoring trap leads us to give disproportionate weight to the first information we receive. The status-quo trap biases us toward maintaining the current situation—even when better alternatives exist. The sunk-cost trap inclines us to perpetuate the mistakes of the past. The confirming-evidence trap leads us to seek out information supporting an existing predilection and to discount opposing information. The framing trap occurs when we misstate a problem, undermining the entire decision-making process. The overconfidence trap makes us overestimate the accuracy of our forecasts. The prudence trap leads us to be overcautious when we make estimates about uncertain events. And the recallability trap prompts us to give undue weight to recent, dramatic events. The best way to avoid all the traps is awareness: Forewarned is forearmed. But executives can also take other simple steps to protect themselves and their organizations from these mental lapses to ensure that their important business decisions are sound and reliable.

In this article, we examine a number of well-documented psychological traps that are particularly likely to undermine business decisions. In addition to reviewing the causes and manifestations of these traps, we offer some specific ways managers can guard against them. It's important to remember, though, that the best defense is always awareness. Executives who attempt to familiarize themselves with these traps and the diverse forms they take will be better able to ensure that the decisions they make are sound and that the recommendations proposed by subordinates or associates are reliable.

The Anchoring Trap

How would you answer these two questions?

- Is the population of Turkey greater than 35 million?

- What's your best estimate of Turkey's population?

If you're like most people, the figure of 35 million cited in the first question (a figure we chose arbitrarily) influenced your answer to the second question. Over the years, we've posed those questions to many groups of people. In half the cases, we used 35 million in the first question; in the other half, we used 100 million. Without fail, the answers to the second question increase by many millions when the larger figure is used in the first question. This simple test illustrates the common and often pernicious mental phenomenon known as *anchoring*. When considering a decision, the mind gives disproportionate weight to the first information it receives. Initial impressions, estimates, or data anchor subsequent thoughts and judgments.

Anchors take many guises. They can be as simple and seemingly innocuous as a comment offered by a colleague or a statistic appearing in the morning newspaper. They can be as insidious as a stereotype about a person's skin color, accent, or dress. In business, one of the most common types of anchors is a past event or trend. A marketer attempting to project the sales of a product for the coming year often begins by looking at the sales volumes for past years. The old numbers become anchors, which the forecaster then adjusts based on other factors. This approach, while it may lead to a reasonably accurate estimate, tends to give too much weight to past events and not enough weight to other factors. In situations characterized by rapid changes in the marketplace, historical anchors can lead to poor forecasts and, in turn, misguided choices.

Because anchors can establish the terms on which a decision will be made, they are often used as a bargaining tactic by savvy negotiators. Consider the experience of a large consulting firm that was searching for new office space in San Francisco. Working with a commercial real-estate broker, the firm's partners identified a building that met all their criteria, and they set up a meeting with the building's owners. The owners opened the meeting by laying out the terms of a proposed contract: a 10-year lease; an initial monthly price of $2.50 per square foot; annual price increases at the prevailing inflation rate; all interior improvements to be the tenant's responsibility; an option for the tenant to extend the lease for 10 additional years under the same terms. Although the price was at the high end of current market rates, the consultants made a relatively modest counteroffer. They proposed an initial price in the midrange of market rates and asked the owners to share in the renovation expenses, but they accepted all the other terms. The consultants could have been much more aggressive and creative in their counterproposal—reducing the initial price to the low end of market rates, adjusting rates biennially rather than annually, putting a cap on the increases, defining different terms for extending the lease, and so forth—but their thinking was guided by the owners' initial proposal. The consultants had fallen into the anchoring trap, and as a result, they ended up paying a lot more for the space than they had to.

What can you do about it?

The effect of anchors in decision making has been documented in thousands of experiments. Anchors influence the decisions not only of managers but also of accountants and engineers, bankers and lawyers, consultants and stock analysts. No one can avoid their influence; they're just too widespread. But managers who are aware of the dangers of anchors can reduce their impact by using the following techniques:

- Always view a problem from different perspectives. Try using alternative starting points and approaches rather than sticking with the first line of thought that occurs to you.

- Think about the problem on your own before consulting others to avoid becoming anchored by their ideas.

- Be open-minded. Seek information and opinions from a variety of people to widen your frame of reference and to push your mind in fresh directions.

- Be careful to avoid anchoring your advisers, consultants, and others from whom you solicit information and counsel. Tell them as little as possible about your own ideas, estimates, and tentative decisions. If you reveal too much, your own preconceptions may simply come back to you.

- Be particularly wary of anchors in negotiations. Think through your position before any negotiation begins in order to avoid being anchored by the other party's initial proposal. At the same time, look for opportunities to use anchors to your own advantage—if you're the seller, for example, suggest a high, but defensible, price as an opening gambit.

The Status-Quo Trap

We all like to believe that we make decisions rationally and objectively. But the fact is, we all carry biases, and those biases influence the choices we make. Decision makers display, for example, a strong bias toward alternatives that perpetuate the status quo. On a broad scale, we can see this tendency whenever a radically new product is introduced. The first automobiles, revealingly called "horseless carriages," looked very much like the buggies they replaced. The first "electronic newspapers" appearing on the World Wide Web looked very much like their print precursors.

On a more familiar level, you may have succumbed to this bias in your personal financial decisions. People sometimes, for example, inherit shares of stock that they would never have bought themselves. Although it would be a straightforward, inexpensive proposition to sell those shares and put the money into a different investment, a surprising number of people don't sell. They find the status quo comfortable, and they avoid taking action that would upset it. "Maybe I'll rethink it later," they say. But "later" is usually never.

The source of the status-quo trap lies deep within our psyches, in our desire to protect our egos from damage. Breaking from the status quo means taking action, and when we take action, we take responsibility, thus opening ourselves to criticism and to regret. Not surprisingly, we naturally look for reasons to do nothing. Sticking with the status quo represents, in most cases, the safer course because it puts us at less psychological risk.

Many experiments have shown the magnetic attraction of the status quo. In one, a group of people were randomly given one of two gifts of approximately the same value—half received a mug, the other half a Swiss chocolate bar. They were then told that they could easily exchange the gift they received for the other gift. While you might expect that about half would have wanted to make the exchange, only one in 10 actually did. The status quo exerted its power even though it had been arbitrarily established only minutes before.

Other experiments have shown that the more choices you are given, the more pull the status quo has. More people will, for instance, choose the status quo when there are two alternatives to it rather than one: A and B instead of just A. Why? Choosing between A and B requires additional effort; selecting the status quo avoids that effort.

In business, where sins of commission (doing something) tend to be punished much more severely than sins of omission (doing nothing), the status quo holds a particularly strong attraction. Many mergers, for example, founder because the acquiring company avoids taking swift action to impose a new, more appropriate management structure on the acquired company. "Let's not rock the boat right now," the typical reasoning goes. "Let's wait until the situation stabilizes." But as time passes, the existing structure becomes more entrenched, and altering it becomes harder, not easier. Having failed to seize the occasion when change would have been expected, management finds itself stuck with the status quo.

What can you do about it?

First of all, remember that in any given decision, maintaining the status quo may indeed be the best choice, but you don't want to choose it just because it is comfortable. Once you become aware of the status-quo trap, you can use these techniques to lessen its pull:

- Always remind yourself of your objectives and examine how they would be served by the status quo. You may find that elements of the current situation act as barriers to your goals.

- Never think of the status quo as your only alternative. Identify other options and use them as counterbalances, carefully evaluating all the pluses and minuses.

- Ask yourself whether you would choose the status-quo alternative if, in fact, it weren't the status quo.

- Avoid exaggerating the effort or cost involved in switching from the status quo.

- Remember that the desirability of the status quo will change over time. When comparing alternatives, always evaluate them in terms of the future as well as the present.

- If you have several alternatives that are superior to the status quo, don't default to the status quo just because you're having a hard time picking the best alternative. Force yourself to choose.

The Sunk-Cost Trap

Another of our deep-seated biases is to make choices in a way that justifies past choices, even when the past choices no longer seem valid. Most of us have fallen into this trap. We may have refused, for example, to sell a stock or a mutual fund at a loss, forgoing other, more attractive investments. Or we may have poured enormous effort into improving the performance of an employee whom we knew we shouldn't have hired in the first place. Our past decisions become what economists term *sunk costs*—old investments of time or money that are now irrecoverable. We know, rationally, that sunk costs are irrelevant to the present decision, but nevertheless they prey on our minds, leading us to make inappropriate decisions.

Why can't people free themselves from past decisions? Frequently, it's because they are unwilling, consciously or not, to admit to a mistake. Acknowledging a poor decision in one's personal life may be purely a private matter, involving only one's self-esteem, but in business, a bad decision is often a very public matter, inviting critical comments from colleagues or bosses. If you fire a poor performer whom you hired, you're making a public admission of poor judgment. It seems psychologically safer to let him or her stay on, even though that choice only compounds the error.

The sunk-cost bias shows up with disturbing regularity in banking, where it can have particularly dire consequences. When a borrower's business runs into trouble, a lender will often advance additional funds in hopes of providing the business with some breathing room to recover. If the business does have a good chance of coming back, that's a wise investment. Otherwise, it's just throwing good money after bad.

One of us helped a major U.S. bank recover after it made many bad loans to foreign businesses. We found that the bankers responsible for originating the problem loans were far more likely to advance additional funds—repeatedly, in many cases—than were bankers who took over the accounts after the original loans were made. Too often, the original bankers' strategy—and loans—ended in failure. Having been trapped by an escalation of commitment, they had tried, consciously or unconsciously, to protect their earlier, flawed decisions. They had fallen victim to the sunk-cost bias. The bank finally solved the problem by instituting a policy requiring that a loan be immediately reassigned to another banker as soon as any problem arose. The new banker was able to take a fresh, unbiased look at the merit of offering more funds.

Sometimes a corporate culture reinforces the sunk-cost trap. If the penalties for making a decision that leads to an unfavorable outcome are overly severe, managers will be motivated to let failed projects drag on endlessly—in the vain hope that they'll somehow be able to transform them into successes. Executives should recognize that, in an uncertain world where unforeseeable events are common, good decisions can sometimes lead to bad outcomes. By acknowledging that some good ideas will end in failure, executives will encourage people to cut their losses rather than let them mount.

What can you do about it?

For all decisions with a history, you will need to make a conscious effort to set aside any sunk costs—whether psychological or economic—that will muddy your thinking about the choice at hand. Try these techniques:

- Seek out and listen carefully to the views of people who were uninvolved with the earlier decisions and who are hence unlikely to be committed to them.

- Examine why admitting to an earlier mistake distresses you. If the problem lies in your own wounded self-esteem, deal with it head-on. Remind yourself that even smart choices can have bad consequences, through no fault of the original decision maker, and that even the best and most experienced managers are not immune to errors in judgment. Remember the wise words of Warren Buffett: "When you find yourself in a hole, the best thing you can do is stop digging."

- Be on the lookout for the influence of sunk-cost biases in the decisions and recommendations made by your subordinates. Reassign responsibilities when necessary.

- Don't cultivate a failure-fearing culture that leads employees to perpetuate their mistakes. In rewarding people, look at the quality of their decision making (taking into account what was known at the time their decisions were made), not just the quality of the outcomes.

The Confirming-Evidence Trap

Imagine that you're the president of a successful midsize U.S. manufacturer considering whether to call off a planned plant expansion. For a while you've been concerned that your company won't be able to sustain the rapid pace of growth of its exports. You fear that the value of the U.S. dollar will strengthen in coming months, making your goods more costly for overseas consumers and dampening demand. But before you put the brakes on the plant expansion, you decide to call up an acquaintance, the chief executive of a similar company that recently mothballed a new factory, to check her reasoning. She presents a strong case that other currencies are about to weaken significantly against the dollar. What do you do?

You'd better not let that conversation be the clincher, because you've probably just fallen victim to the confirming-evidence bias. This bias leads us to seek out information that supports our existing instinct or point of view while avoiding information that contradicts it. What, after all, did you expect your acquaintance to give, other than a strong argument in favor of her own decision? The confirming-evidence bias affects not only where we go to collect evidence but also how we interpret the evidence we do receive, leading us to give too much weight to supporting information and too little to conflicting information.

In one psychological study of this phenomenon, two groups—one opposed to and one supporting capital punishment—each read two reports of carefully conducted research on the effectiveness of the death penalty as a deterrent to crime. One report concluded that the death penalty was effective; the other concluded it was not. Despite being exposed to solid scientific information supporting counterarguments, the members of both groups became even more convinced of the validity of their own position after reading both reports. They automatically accepted the supporting information and dismissed the conflicting information.

There are two fundamental psychological forces at work here. The first is our tendency to subconsciously decide what we want to do before we figure out why we want to do it. The second is our inclination to be more engaged by things we like than by things we dislike—a tendency well documented even in babies. Naturally, then, we are drawn to information that supports our subconscious leanings.

What can you do about it?

It's not that you shouldn't make the choice you're subconsciously drawn to. It's just that you want to be sure it's the smart choice. You need to put it to the test. Here's how:

- Always check to see whether you are examining all the evidence with equal rigor. Avoid the tendency to accept confirming evidence without question.

- Get someone you respect to play devil's advocate, to argue against the decision you're contemplating. Better yet, build the counterarguments yourself. What's the strongest reason to do something else? The second strongest reason? The third? Consider the position with an open mind.

- Be honest with yourself about your motives. Are you really gathering information to help you make a smart choice, or are you just looking for evidence confirming what you think you'd like to do?

- In seeking the advice of others, don't ask leading questions that invite confirming evidence. And if you find that an adviser always seems to support your point of view, find a new adviser. Don't surround yourself with yes-men.

The Framing Trap

The first step in making a decision is to frame the question. It's also one of the most dangerous steps. The way a problem is framed can profoundly influence the choices you make. In a case involving automobile insurance, for example, framing made a $200 million difference. To reduce insurance costs, two neighboring states, New Jersey and Pennsylvania, made similar changes in their laws. Each state gave drivers a new option: By accepting a limited right to sue, they could lower their premiums. But the two states framed the choice in very different ways: In New Jersey, you automatically got the limited right to sue unless you specified otherwise; in Pennsylvania, you got the full right to sue unless you specified otherwise. The different frames established different status quos, and, not surprisingly, most consumers defaulted to the status quo. As a result, in New Jersey about 80% of drivers chose the limited right to sue, but in Pennsylvania only 25% chose it. Because of the way it framed the choice, Pennsylvania failed to gain approximately $200 million in expected insurance and litigation savings.

The framing trap can take many forms, and as the insurance example shows, it is often closely related to other psychological traps. A frame can establish the status quo or introduce an anchor. It can highlight sunk costs or lead you toward confirming evidence. Decision researchers have documented two types of frames that distort decision making with particular frequency.

Frames as gains versus losses

In a study patterned after a classic experiment by decision researchers Daniel Kahneman and Amos Tversky, one of us posed the following problem to a group of insurance professionals:

> *You are a marine property adjuster charged with minimizing the loss of cargo on three insured barges that sank yesterday off the coast of Alaska. Each barge holds $200,000 worth of cargo, which will be lost if not salvaged within 72 hours. The owner of a local marine-salvage company gives you two options, both of which will cost the same:*
> *   ***Plan A:*** *This plan will save the cargo of one of the three barges, worth $200,000.*
> *   ***Plan B:*** *This plan has a one-third probability of saving the cargo on all three barges, worth $600,000, but has a two-thirds probability of saving nothing.*
> *   *Which plan would you choose?*

If you are like 71% of the respondents in the study, you chose the "less risky" Plan A, which will save one barge for sure. Another group in the study, however, was asked to choose between alternatives C and D:

> *   ***Plan C:*** *This plan will result in the loss of two of the three cargoes, worth $400,000.*
> *   ***Plan D:*** *This plan has a two-thirds probability of resulting in the loss of all three cargoes and the entire $600,000 but has a one-third probability of losing no cargo.*

Faced with this choice, 80% of these respondents preferred Plan D.

The pairs of alternatives are, of course, precisely equivalent— Plan A is the same as Plan C, and Plan B is the same as Plan D— they've just been framed in different ways. The strikingly different responses reveal that people are risk averse when a problem is posed in terms of gains (barges saved) but risk seeking when a problem is posed in terms of avoiding losses (barges lost). Furthermore, they tend to adopt the frame as it is presented to them rather than restating the problem in their own way.

Framing with different reference points

The same problem can also elicit very different responses when frames use different reference points. Let's say you have $2,000 in your checking account and you are asked the following question:

Would you accept a fifty-fifty chance of either losing $300 or winning $500?

Would you accept the chance? What if you were asked this question:

Would you prefer to keep your checking account balance of $2,000 or to accept a fifty-fifty chance of having either $1,700 or $2,500 in your account?

Once again, the two questions pose the same problem. While your answers to both questions should, rationally speaking, be the same, studies have shown that many people would refuse the fifty-fifty chance in the first question but accept it in the second.

Their different reactions result from the different reference points presented in the two frames. The first frame, with its reference point of zero, emphasizes incremental gains and losses, and the thought of losing triggers a conservative response in many people's minds. The second frame, with its reference point of $2,000, puts things into perspective by emphasizing the real financial impact of the decision.

What can you do about it?

A poorly framed problem can undermine even the best-considered decision. But any adverse effect of framing can be limited by taking the following precautions:

- Don't automatically accept the initial frame, whether it was formulated by you or by someone else. Always try to reframe the problem in various ways. Look for distortions caused by the frames.

- Try posing problems in a neutral, redundant way that combines gains and losses or embraces different reference points. For example: Would you accept a fifty-fifty chance of either losing $300, resulting in a bank balance of $1,700, or winning $500, resulting in a bank balance of $2,500?

- Think hard throughout your decision-making process about the framing of the problem. At points throughout the process, particularly near the end, ask yourself how your thinking might change if the framing changed.

- When others recommend decisions, examine the way they framed the problem. Challenge them with different frames.

The Estimating and Forecasting Traps

Most of us are adept at making estimates about time, distance, weight, and volume. That's because we're constantly making judgments about these variables and getting quick feedback about the accuracy of those judgments. Through daily practice, our minds become finely calibrated.

Making estimates or forecasts about uncertain events, however, is a different matter. While managers continually make such estimates and forecasts, they rarely get clear feedback about their accuracy. If you judge, for example, that the likelihood of the price of oil falling to less than $15 a barrel one year hence is about 40% and the price does indeed fall to that level, you can't tell whether you were right or wrong about the probability you estimated. The only way to gauge your accuracy would be to keep track of many, many similar judgments to see if, after the fact, the events you thought had a 40% chance of occurring actually did occur 40% of the time. That would require a great deal of data, carefully tracked over a long period of time. Weather forecasters and bookmakers have the opportunities and incentives to maintain such records, but the rest of us don't. As a result, our minds never become calibrated for making estimates in the face of uncertainty.

All of the traps we've discussed so far can influence the way we make decisions when confronted with uncertainty. But there's another set of traps that can have a particularly distorting effect in uncertain situations because they cloud our ability to assess probabilities. Let's look at three of the most common of these uncertainty traps.

The overconfidence trap

Even though most of us are not very good at making estimates or forecasts, we actually tend to be overconfident about our accuracy. That can lead to errors in judgment and, in turn, bad decisions. In one series of tests, people were asked to forecast the next week's closing value for the Dow Jones Industrial Average. To account for uncertainty, they were then asked to estimate a range within which the closing value would likely fall. In picking the top number of the range, they were asked to choose a high estimate they thought had only a 1% chance of being exceeded by the closing value. Similarly, for the bottom end, they were told to pick a low estimate for which they thought there would be only a 1% chance of the closing value falling below it. If they were good at judging their forecasting accuracy, you'd expect the participants to be wrong only about 2% of the time. But hundreds of tests have shown that the actual Dow Jones averages fell outside the forecast ranges 20% to 30% of the time. Overly confident about the accuracy of their predictions, most people set too narrow a range of possibilities.

Think of the implications for business decisions, in which major initiatives and investments often hinge on ranges of estimates. If managers underestimate the high end or overestimate the low end of a crucial variable, they may miss attractive opportunities or expose themselves to far greater risk than they realize. Much money has been wasted on ill-fated product-development projects because managers did not accurately account for the possibility of market failure.

The prudence trap

Another trap for forecasters takes the form of overcautiousness, or prudence. When faced with high-stakes decisions, we tend to adjust our estimates or forecasts "just to be on the safe side." Many years ago, for example, one of the Big Three U.S. automakers was deciding how many of a new-model car to produce in anticipation of its busiest sales season. The market-planning department, responsible for the decision, asked other departments to supply forecasts of key variables such as anticipated sales, dealer inventories, competitor actions, and costs. Knowing the purpose of the estimates, each department slanted its forecast to favor building more cars—"just to be safe." But the market planners took the numbers at face value and then made their own "just to be safe" adjustments. Not surprisingly, the number of cars produced far exceeded demand, and the company took six months to sell off the surplus, resorting in the end to promotional pricing.

Policymakers have gone so far as to codify overcautiousness in formal decision procedures. An extreme example is the methodology of "worst-case analysis," which was once popular in the design of weapons systems and is still used in certain engineering and regulatory settings. Using this approach, engineers designed weapons to operate under the worst possible combination of circumstances, even though the odds of those circumstances actually coming to pass were infinitesimal. Worst-case analysis added enormous costs with no practical benefit (in fact, it often backfired by touching off an arms race), proving that too much prudence can sometimes be as dangerous as too little.

The recallability trap

Even if we are neither overly confident nor unduly prudent, we can still fall into a trap when making estimates or forecasts. Because we frequently base our predictions about future events on our memory of past events, we can be overly influenced by dramatic events—those that leave a strong impression on our memory. We all, for example, exaggerate the probability of rare but catastrophic occurrences such as plane crashes because they get disproportionate attention in the media. A dramatic or traumatic event in your own life can also distort your thinking. You will assign a higher probability to traffic accidents if you have passed one on the way to work, and you will assign a higher chance of someday dying of cancer yourself if a close friend has died of the disease.

In fact, anything that distorts your ability to recall events in a balanced way will distort your probability assessments. In one experiment, lists of well-known men and women were read to different groups of people. Unbeknownst to the subjects, each list had an equal number of men and women, but on some lists the men were more famous than the women while on others the women were more famous. Afterward, the participants were asked to estimate the percentages of men and women on each list. Those who had heard the list with the more famous men thought there were more men on the list, while those who had heard the one with the more famous women thought there were more women.

Corporate lawyers often get caught in the recallability trap when defending liability suits. Their decisions about whether to settle a claim or take it to court usually hinge on their assessments of the possible outcomes of a trial. Because the media tend to aggressively publicize massive damage awards (while ignoring other, far more common trial outcomes), lawyers can overestimate the probability of a large award for the plaintiff. As a result, they offer larger settlements than are actually warranted.

What can you do about it?

The best way to avoid the estimating and forecasting traps is to take a very disciplined approach to making forecasts and judging probabilities. For each of the three traps, some additional precautions can be taken:

- To reduce the effects of overconfidence in making estimates, always start by considering the extremes, the low and high ends of the possible range of values. This will help you avoid being anchored by an initial estimate. Then challenge your estimates of the extremes. Try to imagine circumstances where the actual figure would fall below your low or above your high, and adjust your range accordingly. Challenge the estimates of your subordinates and advisers in a similar fashion. They're also susceptible to overconfidence.

- To avoid the prudence trap, always state your estimates honestly and explain to anyone who will be using them that they have not been adjusted. Emphasize the need for honest input to anyone who will be supplying you with estimates. Test estimates over a reasonable range to assess their impact. Take a second look at the more sensitive estimates.

- To minimize the distortion caused by variations in recallability, carefully examine all your assumptions to ensure they're not unduly influenced by your memory. Get actual statistics whenever possible. Try not to be guided by impressions.

Forewarned Is Forearmed

When it comes to business decisions, there's rarely such a thing as a no-brainer. Our brains are always at work, sometimes, unfortunately, in ways that hinder rather than help us. At every stage of the decision-making process, misperceptions, biases, and other tricks of the mind can influence the choices we make. Highly complex and important decisions are the most prone to distortion because they tend to involve the most assumptions, the most estimates, and the most inputs from the most people. The higher the stakes, the higher the risk of being caught in a psychological trap.

The traps we've reviewed can all work in isolation. But, even more dangerous, they can work in concert, amplifying one another. A dramatic first impression might anchor our thinking, and then we might selectively seek out confirming evidence to justify our initial inclination. We make a hasty decision, and that decision establishes a new status quo. As our sunk costs mount, we become trapped, unable to find a propitious time to seek out a new and possibly better course. The psychological miscues cascade, making it harder and harder to choose wisely.

As we said at the outset, the best protection against all psychological traps—in isolation or in combination—is awareness. Forewarned is forearmed. Even if you can't eradicate the distortions ingrained into the way your mind works, you can build tests and disciplines into your decision-making process that can uncover errors in thinking before they become errors in judgment. And taking action to understand and avoid psychological traps can have the added benefit of increasing your confidence in the choices you make.

Originally published in January 2006. Reprint R0601K

Stop Overthinking and Start Trusting Your Gut

by Melody Wilding

Hunch, instinct, deeper knowing: There are many names for gut feelings, or the ability to immediately understand something without conscious reasoning. In other words, answers and solutions come to you, but you may not be aware of exactly why or how.

In the age of big data, trusting your gut often gets a bad rap. *Intuition*—the term used in research to refer to gut feelings—is frequently dismissed as mystical or unreliable. While it's true that intuition can be fallible, studies show that pairing gut feelings with analytical thinking helps you make better, faster, and more accurate decisions and gives you more confidence in your choices than relying on intellect alone. This is especially true when you're overthinking or when there is no single clear-cut, "correct" option.

In fact, surveys of top executives show that a majority of leaders leverage their feelings and experience when handling crises. Even the U.S. Navy has invested millions of dollars in helping sailors and marines refine their sixth sense, precisely because intuition can supersede intellect in high-stakes situations like the battlefield.

The Science Behind Your Gut Feelings

Despite popular belief, there's a deep neurological basis for intuition. Scientists call the stomach the "second brain" for a reason. There's a vast neural network of 100 million neurons lining your entire digestive tract. That's more neurons than are found in the spinal cord, which points to the gut's incredible processing abilities.

When you approach a decision intuitively, your brain works in tandem with your gut to quickly assess all your memories, past learnings, personal needs, and preferences and then makes the wisest decision given the context. In this way, intuition is a form of emotional and experiential data that leaders need to value.

Even if you're not consciously using your intuition, you still probably experience benefits from it every day. Everyone knows what it feels like to have a pit in your stomach as you weigh a decision. That's the gut talking loud and clear. If you're a manager, for example, getting a read on your direct reports allows you to sense when they're demotivated and to take steps to reengage them. Similarly, doing a gut check on a product design can steer your creative process in the right direction.

How to Leverage Your Intuition in Decision-Making

Leaders who identify as highly sensitive have stronger gut feelings than most but have also been discouraged from using this sensory data. The trait of high sensitivity contributes to

Idea in Brief

The Challenge

Overthinking can paralyze your decision-making and drain your mental energy. Many professionals get stuck in cycles of analysis and self-doubt, missing opportunities and delaying action.

The Insight

While thoughtful reflection has its place, intuition—when informed by experience—can be a powerful guide. Learning to trust your gut doesn't mean ignoring data; it means recognizing when you have enough insight to move forward with confidence. Practice tuning into your instincts and recognizing patterns from past experiences. Set time limits for decisions, embrace imperfection, and reframe mistakes as learning opportunities.

The Implications

Professionals who balance analysis with intuition make faster, more confident decisions and free up cognitive space for creativity and growth. Building self-trust takes practice, but it starts with small, intentional steps.

perceiving, processing, and synthesizing information more deeply, including data about others' emotional worlds. This means your intuition is more highly developed than most other people's because you're constantly adding new data to your bank of knowledge about the world and yourself. The only problem is that you've probably been taught to devalue this strength in yourself.

The good news is that intuition is like a muscle—it can be strengthened with intentional practice. Here are a few ways to begin leveraging your intuition as a helpful decision-making tool in your career.

Discern gut feeling from fear

Fear tends to be accompanied by bodily sensations of constricting or minimizing. You may feel tense, panicky, or desperate. Fear has a pushing energy, as if you're trying to force something or are selecting an option because you want to avoid a threat, rejection, or punishment. Fear also tends to be dominated by self-critical thoughts that urge you to hide, conform, or compromise yourself.

Intuition, on the other hand, has a pulling energy, as if your choice is moving you toward your best interest, even if that means pursuing a risk or moving more slowly than others. This is usually accompanied by feelings of excitement and anticipation or ease and contentment. Physically, gut feelings tend to cause your body to relax. With intuition, your inner voice is more grounded and wise, like a good mentor.

Start by making minor decisions

Choose an outfit that calls to you without weighing too many variables. Raise your hand and speak up in a meeting without censoring yourself. Taking quick, decisive actions with small consequences gets you comfortable using your intuition. By starting small, you mitigate feelings of overwhelm and can gradually step your way up to larger, higher-pressure decisions with greater self-trust. This approach is effective because it builds your distress tolerance, or your ability to emotionally regulate in the face of discomfort.

Test-drive your choices

When you're first starting to use your intuition, decisions may not come to you quickly. Instead of overthinking, role-play your choices. For two or three days, act as if you've chosen Option A— for example, an opportunity in a new industry. Observe how you think and feel. Then, for another two or three days, try on Option B, say, staying on your current career path. At the end of the experiment, take stock of your reactions. Simulating the outcome can tell you a lot about the outcome you really want and which decision would be best for you. You can also try flipping a coin and seeing how you feel about the answer. If heads means declining a big deal, do you feel joy and relief? Or worry and dread?

Try the snap-judgment test

Relying on rapid cognition, or thin-slicing, can allow your brain to make decisions without overthinking and can help strengthen your trust in your gut. Give this a try with the snap-judgment test. On a piece of paper, write a question such as, "Will taking the promotion make me happy?" List yes or no below the question. Leave a pen nearby. After a few hours, come back to the paper and immediately circle your answer. It might not be an answer you like, especially if the question is a big one, but there's a good chance that you forced yourself to respond honestly.

Fall back on your values

Your core values represent what's most important to you. Examples include freedom, diversity, stability, family, or calmness. Let's say you're feeling agitated after a long day at work when nothing went your way. Your core values can help you pinpoint the source of your frustration and understand it more clearly. For example, perhaps you value honesty and what's causing tension is that you're not sharing your true feelings on an important issue. Using your values, you can check in to figure out what feels off internally and to gain perspective on the situation.

Take a moment today to reflect on what your top one to three values may be. The next time you find yourself struggling to make a decision, ask yourself, "Which action or decision brings me closer to those core values?" Going within can help dissolve the internal tension that leads to mental loops.

Finally, keep in mind that intuition can't flourish in busy, stressful environments. Give your mind the space to wander and make connections. Remember, while intuition is not perfect, it's a decision-making tool you're likely underutilizing at the moment. Give these strategies a try, and you'll probably be surprised to find that your gut is a more powerful tool than you realized.

Adapted from "How to Stop Overthinking and Start Trusting Your Gut" on hbr.org, March 10, 2022. Reprint H06WHX

3

Fooled by Experience

by Emre Soyer and Robin M. Hogarth

We rely on the weight of experience to make judgments and decisions. We interpret the past—what we've seen and what we've been told—to chart a course for the future, secure in the wisdom of our insights. After all, didn't our ability to make sense of what we've been through get us where we are now? It's reasonable that we go back to the same well to make new decisions.

It could also be a mistake.

Experience seems like a reliable guide, yet sometimes it fools us instead of making us wiser.

The problem is that we view the past through numerous filters that distort our perceptions. As a result, our interpretations of experience are biased, and the judgments and decisions we base on those interpretations can be misguided. Even so, we persist in believing that we have gleaned the correct insights from our own experience and from the accounts of other people.

If our goal is to improve decision making, we can use our knowledge of those filters to understand just what our experience has to teach us. Distilling a wide range of research on the subject, we focus in this article on the biases that result from three types of filters: the business environment, which favors the observation of outcomes (especially successes) over the processes that lead to them; our circle of advisers, who may be censoring the information they share with us; and our own limited reasoning abilities. We also consider techniques for overcoming those biases.

We Focus on What We Can See

In the business environment, the outcomes of decisions are highly visible, readily available for us to observe and judge. But the details of the decision process, which we can control far more than the result, typically don't catch our attention. If the aim is to learn from experience—mistakes as well as successes—acknowledging that process is crucial.

Imagine that two firms use the same risky strategy, but one gets lucky and prospers while the other doesn't. We celebrate the first one and condemn the second—a response that disregards the underlying causes. The tendency to overreward the results of a decision and underreward its quality is known as the outcome bias.

This bias can influence our actions in subtle ways. A good outcome can lead us to stick with a questionable strategy, and a bad outcome can cause us to change or discard a strategy that may still be worthwhile. For example, in the NBA, coaches "are more likely to revise their strategy after a loss than a win—even for narrow losses, which are uninformative about team effectiveness," a recent *Management Science* article shows.[1]

A focus on outcomes can also influence our sense of ethics. A Harvard Business School working paper finds that "the same behaviors produce more ethical condemnation when they

Idea in Brief

The Status Quo

Experience: We think of it as our guide, a reliable source of insight, and the foundation of our expertise. As we make decisions, we rely on our experience and on what advisers and confidants tell us about theirs.

The Problem

We view our experience through multiple filters that distort reality, limiting our ability to figure out what's actually going on around us. As a consequence, our experiences fool us instead of making us wiser.

The Solution

We can base our decisions on a clearer view of the world if we focus not just on outcomes but on the processes that lead to them; learn from near misses; encourage disagreement and the search for disconfirming evidence; and broaden our perspective.

happen to produce bad rather than good outcomes, even if the outcomes are determined by chance."[2] In other words, if everything turns out OK, we're more likely to think that the decision was not just effective but also morally sound.

Our attention to outcomes—and disregard of the processes that create them—makes solutions seem more valuable than preventive actions. A decision maker who solves a burning problem can be identified and rewarded, while one who takes action to avoid the same problem is far harder to spot.

Among outcomes, successes are more visible than failures. The business world is awash with success stories: The latest bestsellers, the biggest startup, and winning corporate strategies are widely trumpeted, while failures quietly disappear.

Relying on stories of successes and on analyses of what those successes have in common is as unreliable a practice as it is popular. In an article in *Organization Science*, Jerker Denrell points out that observing the common managerial practices of existing organizations can mislead us in a couple of ways.[3] First, failures can share some of the same traits as successes. Second, if certain factors always lead to failure, we won't be able to discover them by studying only successes. Approach with caution any list that purports to reveal, for instance, "10 common traits of successful companies"—whether it is punctuated with an exclamation point or comes with the seriousness of a legitimate study.

Ignoring failures has another effect. In *Fooled by Randomness,* Nassim Nicholas Taleb argues that doing so masks the failure rate. If the rate is high, chances are there is no magic formula for success. And if there's no magic formula, then a manager can't be faulted for missing it. By concealing the prevalence of failures, the environment makes it more difficult for us to learn from them. Instead, we are fooled into thinking that we have more control over success than we actually do.

We Trust Our Circle of Advisers

Honest feedback—an unbiased, undistorted assessment of one's experience—is essential for improving decisions. Yet decision makers are often surrounded by individuals who have incentives to feed them censored and self-serving information—and these people are not necessarily a crowd of yes-men.

Censorship is a powerful tool for influencing opinion. Restricting the information that reaches decision makers installs a strong bias in their perceptions. Even if we are aware of the existence of censors, it can be difficult to think beyond the immediately available information. Our intuitions are often shaped by the evidence we recall, no matter its relevance—a tendency cognitive scientists call the availability bias.

Individuals who are hoping for a raise, a promotion, or some other benefit may well choose to deliver partial and insincere feedback, omitting anything negative about a decision maker's performance. As the organizational psychologist Lynn Offermann argues in "When Followers Become Toxic" (HBR, January 2004), leaders run the danger of being "surrounded by followers who fool them with flattery and isolate them from uncomfortable realities." In this way, flattery can be an especially powerful filter.

But your trusted advisers aren't necessarily aiming to ingratiate themselves with you; they may just be trying to conform. One powerful way to do that is to agree with you. It is much easier to conform to others' opinions than to voice objections. If all your advisers follow that approach, you won't have any dissenters.

Your demeanor can make matters worse. Shooting the messenger doesn't facilitate healthy communication. Indeed, welcoming criticism is hard, especially for people with high status.

Censorship and a desire for conformity give decision makers a distorted view of their strategic competence, a bias that can result in their downfall. A recent article in *Administrative Science Quarterly* suggests that such misperceptions may reduce "the likelihood that CEOs will initiate needed strategic change in response to poor firm performance," which, of course, can lead to their dismissal.[4]

Executives who are surrounded by people who agree with them may also experience decreased creativity and problem-solving abilities. Conceiving an idea, a strategy, or a methodology is rarely a solo act. A successful creative endeavor involves input from a diverse set of people. If everyone is simply trying to conform, the group cannot benefit from people's backgrounds, perspectives, and experiences.

We Overvalue Our Own Experience

We can't place all the blame for our distorted view of the world on the environment and our inner circle. Some of the blame lies with us. Our own reasoning abilities can sabotage how we collect information and evaluate evidence. We end up learning the wrong lessons from our experience—even when it's possible to learn the right ones.

One issue is that we tend to search for and use evidence that confirms our beliefs and hypotheses, and we gloss over or ignore information that contradicts them—an exercise of selectively building and interpreting experience known as the confirmation bias. We can easily support our beloved superstitions, spurious correlations, and bogus connections. This natural tendency of the human mind hinders competent decision making.

Some see external, information-rich big data as a possible remedy, but data is subject to the same kinds of bias. If analysts cherry-pick information to suit managers' expectations, managers will be reassured about their decisions and see no need to improve them. And once misleading insights are data approved, they are even harder to challenge.

Another issue is our memory. The philosopher John Stuart Mill wrote in *On Liberty,* "There are many truths of which the full meaning cannot be realized, until personal experience has brought it home." Mill's sentiment assumes that we record and remember events accurately. We don't.

In addition to the poor quality and reliability of our memory of experience, there is the crucial problem of quantity. The issue is sampling variability: A manager's personal experience is inevitably based on small samples of incidents that are most likely unrepresentative of the whole context; there is no way that any one manager can experience the entire range of possibilities. Differences among incidents may be due to unknown factors or randomness. If managers read too much into those differences, they may be fooled into seeing patterns that do not actually exist and illusory relationships among unrelated variables. Our belief in the relationship between the past and the future also can interfere with our view of the world. Predictions based on experience make the crucial assumption that the future will resemble the past. One of us, Robin Hogarth, has done extensive research on how human intuition fares in prediction tasks. The findings suggest that not even experts with a tremendous amount of experience are proficient in foreseeing economic, social, and technological developments.

Managers should be aware that just because something seems obvious after the fact does not mean that it could have been predicted. Decision makers often fall into this hindsight bias, which can lead to overconfidence and illusions of control. When it comes to effective decision making, not knowing that you cannot predict is a bigger sin than not being able to predict.

How Not to Be Fooled

The following techniques can uncover the real lessons experience offers. None are easy, but making the effort to adopt them can help you base decisions on a clearer view of the world.

Sample failure

Failures and the processes that lead to them are doomed to stay in the dark unless special occasions are created to bring them to light. It is not easy for managers to share their experiences of defeat. One exception is Paul Biggar, a founder of *Newstilt*, who posted a detailed account of the fall of the news website, which stayed open for just two months in 2010. To give more people the opportunity to share their stories of failure, a group of entrepreneurs has been organizing FailCon, a conference dedicated to giving visibility to experiences that would otherwise remain hidden.

To identify what could be done better in the future, companies can also conduct decision postmortems to analyze underlying processes. Of course, the goal of learning must dominate the natural tendency to assign blame.

Don't miss near misses

Another oft-ignored event is the near miss—a failure that's disguised as a success, but only because there are generally no dire consequences.

An executive at a chemical company told us of a near miss when a machine malfunctioned at a plant, causing a sudden burst of extremely hot gas. Luckily, no workers were nearby, but a quick inquiry revealed that some of the workers in the plant hadn't been wearing protective gear at the time of the incident, even though they are required to put it on the minute they step onto the premises. Exposure to the gas without the safety gear would have resulted in serious physical injury.

It might be easy to dismiss this episode as unimportant, since no one was hurt. But doing so would deprive the company of an opportunity to learn a valuable lesson without having to suffer dreadful consequences. Ironically, ignoring this near disaster—as so often happens—would lead workers to perceive it as inconsequential and thus would help perpetuate the same dangerous behavior.

As Catherine Tinsley, Robin Dillon, and Peter Madsen have shown in "How to Avoid Catastrophe" (HBR, April 2011), risk-free,

Why learning from experience is complicated

Behaviors	Consequences	Remedies
We focus on outcomes, especially successes.	We don't study the process leading up to an outcome. We underestimate the role of chance. We change strategies for the wrong reasons. Solving problems is rewarded; preventing them is not.	Deliberately study failures. Conduct postmortems on decision processes. Learn from near misses. Reward people who prevent problems from occurring.
Advisers censor what they tell us.	Our view of our strategic competence becomes distorted. People feel compelled to agree with the group. The group becomes less creative.	Build a brain trust with differing points of view on strategic questions. Find a confidant who will disagree with you. Create risk-free, anonymous reporting channels.
We focus on evidence that confirms our beliefs.	We continue to base decisions on spurious correlations and connections. Data analysts and consultants may feel compelled to tell us what we want to hear.	Actively look for disconfirming evidence. Imagine the decision went badly, then figure out probable reasons. Don't tip your hand to data scientists or other experts brought in to help.
We rely on our faulty memories, our limited experience, and our misguided belief that the future will resemble the past.	We see patterns that don't exist. We try to predict things that can't be predicted. Unexpected events are seen as hindrances rather than opportunities.	Seek out caveats that would endanger your mission. Imagine more than one possible scenario. Acknowledge the role of luck. Embrace serendipity.

anonymous reporting channels can reduce close calls and disastrous mistakes in many sectors.

Pursue prevention

Recognizing a potential problem requires a different approach than *solving* an actual problem. One strategy is to harness employees' collective talents by allowing people to raise concerns about the firm's operations. Many companies' incentive mechanisms work exactly to the contrary, and employees often hesitate to speak up for fear of reprisal or being labeled a nuisance. But the signs of a blunder can be picked up more easily by lower-level managers and personnel who deal with daily operations than by their senior colleagues. Employees should be made to feel comfortable reporting issues to the very top—even obliged to do so.

Disagree

As Peter Drucker wrote, "The first rule in decision making is that one does not make a decision unless there is disagreement." To devise healthy strategies, executives need to hear many perspectives, including feedback that is critical of their own actions. Executives should surround themselves with people from diverse backgrounds and promote independent thinking in their team. Many executives task certain coworkers, friends, or family members with speaking frankly on important matters.

Ed Catmull, the president of Pixar and Walt Disney Animation Studios, stresses the importance of building a brain trust, a group of advisers who will deflate egos and voice unpopular opinions. He argues in his September 2008 HBR article that disagreements in meetings end up benefiting everyone in the long run, because "it's far better to learn about problems from colleagues when there's still time to fix them than from the audience after it's too late."

Disconfirm

Rather than finding clues that corroborate your hunch—all too easy in an information-rich world—start by asking yourself how you could know you were, in fact, wrong. What evidence would contradict your belief and how likely is it that you would see it? One technique is to use this thought experiment: Imagine that you are already in the future and things have not turned out as you had hoped. Now use your new hindsight to ask how this might have happened.

If you do go the route of using big data, refrain from revealing your hopes and dreams to the data scientists you hire to collect and mine information. Ask questions in a way that prompts them to look for caveats that would endanger your mission but that doesn't reveal what you actually hope they'll find.

Lose focus

It may seem that to mine our experience for valuable lessons, we must focus on the experiences we think really matter. In fact, a narrow perspective can be a serious impediment. In *The Luck Factor,* the psychologist Richard Wiseman shows that when people focus too much on an issue or a task, they inevitably miss out on unexpected opportunities. For a firm, spotting those opportunities is vital. A company that directs its R&D efforts on a single domain, a startup that uses only a few channels of communication, or a manager who employs only people from a certain background will not be able to cope well with the complexity of today's business environment.

Being open to the unexpected is also crucial for individuals. A wide perspective can help, giving new meaning to our varied experiences and allowing us to learn from them and draw on them in surprising ways. The result is often serendipitous discovery and innovation. Curiosity prompted Alexander Fleming to inspect a moldy petri dish before cleaning it, a move that resulted in the discovery of penicillin. Similarly, a passion for hiking and hunting led George de Mestral to invent Velcro. Seeds that got stuck in his dog's fur gave him the idea for the product.

Managers who acknowledge the role of serendipity and luck have an advantage over those who have illusions of control and are overconfident about the accuracy of their judgments. Change is both inevitable and unpredictable. As Spyros Makridakis, Robin Hogarth, and Anil Gaba argue in *Dance with Chance,* managers who accept that can calibrate their intuitions accordingly and learn to see change as an opportunity rather than a shock. To do so, they must broaden their perspective. Welcoming diverse experiences will help decision makers manage the unknowns ahead and greatly increase the odds of being in the right place at the right time.

. . .

The lessons experience seems to be teaching us, accepted uncritically, should almost never guide our actions. What we learn from experience is typically filtered: by the business environment, by the people around us, and by ourselves. If we keep the filters and their antidotes clearly in mind, we can discover what experience actually has to teach us.

As the late Hillel Einhorn, one of the fathers of behavioral decision theory, asked, "If we believe we can learn from experience, can we also learn that we can't?"

Originally published in May 2015. Reprint R1505E

4

What Makes Strategic Decisions Different

by Phil Rosenzweig

The past decade has seen a wealth of research on decision making, much of it not only useful but also fascinating to read. At the same time, a growing chorus has noted that business executives, in particular, are largely impervious to its lessons. They seem unable to apply those lessons, or perhaps uninterested in doing so. Advances in our understanding of decision making have not been matched by improvements in practice.

Having thought about this puzzle for some time, I suggest that there is a good explanation for the disconnect. It's not that executives lack the desire to make better decisions or that they're in denial about their propensity for error. The problem lies elsewhere. It's that the bulk of the decision-making research published to date applies to one type of decision, and it's not the type that's most challenging for managers. Their most important and most difficult decisions—strategic decisions with consequences for the performance of the company—call for a very different approach.

The fact is that people need to make up their minds in a great variety of circumstances, and it's a source of confusion that the same word, *decision*, is used for all of them. When a grocery store customer encounters an entire aisle of breakfast cereals, we say he has a decision to make. When a high school senior considers which college to attend, we say she is facing a decision. When a poker player weighs whether to raise or fold, that's a decision, too. And when a company faces an opportunity—to enter a new market, acquire another company, or launch a new product—what is required of its management? A decision. The same term is applied to routine as well as complex deliberations, to both small-stakes bets and high-stakes commitments, and to exploratory steps as well as irreversible moves. It stands to reason that insights about decisions in one kind of circumstance might not shed much light on decisions in another. Even worse, they may lead a decision maker astray.

In this article I'll argue that before we can advise people on how to make better strategic decisions, we need to equip them to recognize how decisions differ. For that, we need to break the universe of decisions into a few categories. We can then suggest the best approach for each.

Let me propose a way.

Categorizing Decisions

Decisions vary along two dimensions: control and performance. The first considers how much we can influence the terms of the decision and the outcome. Are we choosing among options presented to us, or can we shape those options? Are we making a onetime judgment, unable to change what happens after the fact, or do we have some control over how things play out once

The Problem

Research has revealed much about how to improve decisions, yet managers make little use of the insights.

The Idea

The fact is, the decisions we make fall into four different categories. The right approach depends on how much control the decision maker has over terms and outcomes, and on whether success will be judged in relative or absolute terms.

The Advice

Managers will make better strategic decisions when they learn to identify which kind they're facing and develop the versatility to change approaches accordingly.

we've made the decision? The second dimension addresses the way we measure success. Is our aim to do well, no matter what anyone else does, or do we need to do better than others? That is, is performance absolute or relative?

There are other ways to think about decisions, of course. Some are made by people acting as individuals and others by people acting as leaders of organizations; some are one-offs while others are part of a sequence, with the results of one letting us improve the next. But as a basic way to understand how decisions differ, control and performance are the two dimensions that matter most. Combining them creates four fields of decisions. (See the exhibit "Four types of decisions.")

1. Making routine choices and judgments

When you go shopping in a supermarket or a department store, you typically pick from the products before you. Those items, perhaps a jug of milk or a jar of jam, are what they are. You have

Four types of decisions

To get better at making decisions, it's important to recognize the different types. Those in the first field of the matrix—where we have no control over outcomes and our performance is absolute (we aren't competing with anyone)—include consumer choices and personal investment decisions. Those in the fourth field—where we can influence outcomes and need to outperform rivals—include the strategic decisions that are most challenging for managers, such as launching a new product or entering a new market.

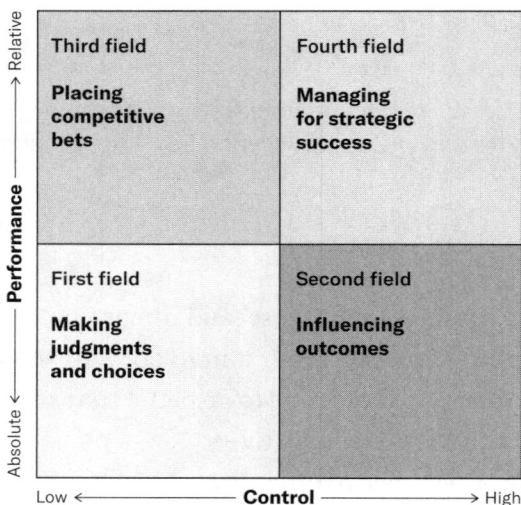

	Low ← Control → High	
Relative	**Third field** **Placing competitive bets**	**Fourth field** **Managing for strategic success**
Absolute	**First field** **Making judgments and choices**	**Second field** **Influencing outcomes**

Performance (vertical axis: Absolute ↔ Relative). Control (horizontal axis: Low ↔ High).

no ability to improve them. Control is low. Moreover, you make the choice that suits you best—it doesn't matter what anyone else is buying. Performance is absolute. The same goes for most personal investment decisions. You may be able to decide which company's shares to buy, but you can't improve their performance after you buy them. You want high returns but aren't trying to do better than others. The goal is to do well, not to finish first in a competition.

In recent years, trailblazing research by cognitive psychologists and behavioral economists has demonstrated that people make decisions in ways that do not conform to the tenets of economic rationality. They exhibit systematic biases. Those findings have shed light on many first-field decisions in particular. For example, we now understand that the way options are framed and presented can shape our purchasing decisions. We know that investors often misunderstand the nature of random events, imagining that several gains indicate that a correction is due or that a string of losses means gains must follow—an error known as the gambler's fallacy. They also fall victim to the sunk-cost fallacy, throwing good money after bad in an effort to recoup what they've lost. For many first-field decisions, research has taught us to be aware of and try to minimize these common biases.

2. Influencing outcomes

Many decisions involve more than selecting among options we cannot improve or making judgments about things we cannot influence. In so much of life, we use our energy and talents to make things happen. Imagine that the task at hand is to determine how long we will need to complete a project. That's a judgment we can control; indeed, it's up to us to get the project done. Here, positive thinking matters. By believing we can do well, perhaps even holding a level of confidence that is by some definitions a bit excessive, we can often improve performance. Optimism isn't useful in picking stocks whose performance we cannot change, but in the second field, where we have the ability to influence outcomes, it can be very important.

Some activities call for us to move between the first and second fields, shifting our mindset back and forth. The approach known as "deliberate practice," which can lead to expert performance (see "The Making of an Expert," by K. Anders

Ericsson, Michael J. Prietula, and Edward T. Cokely, HBR July–August 2007), is based on objective and deliberate thinking before an event, full commitment with a positive attitude while taking action, and then a return to dispassionate analysis after the event—what is known as an after-action review. The ability to shift effectively between mindsets is a crucial element of high performance in many repeated tasks of short duration, from sports to sales.

3. Placing competitive bets

The third field introduces a competitive dimension. Success is no longer a matter of absolute performance but depends on how well you do relative to others. The best decisions must anticipate the moves of rivals. That's the essence of strategic thinking, which Princeton professor Avinash Dixit and Yale professor Barry Nalebuff define as "the art of outdoing an adversary, knowing that the adversary is trying to do the same to you." Investments in stocks are typically first-field decisions, but if you're taking part in a contest where the investor with the highest return takes the prize, you're in the third field. Now you need to make decisions with an eye to what your rivals will do, anticipating their likely moves so that you can have the best chance of winning.

In the third field, guidance comes from the branch of economics that studies competitive dynamics: game theory. Well-known illustrations of game theory include the prisoner's dilemma and the game rock-paper-scissors, in which the winner is determined by the interaction of all players' decisions. Game theory can illuminate areas from price competition to geopolitics, yet it has an important limitation: Players cannot alter the terms of the game. The possible moves are specified, and gains and costs cannot be changed. That's a helpful simplification for purposes of modeling, but it reduces the value for managers. Management, after all, is precisely about influencing outcomes over time. That's why Herbert Simon, in his 1978 Nobel Prize address, commented that for all its sophistication, game theory does not provide "satisfactory descriptions of actual human behavior." An essential aspect of so many crucial decisions is absent.

Decisions in the Fourth Field

The crux of our discussion comes into focus when we consider the fourth field. For these decisions, we can actively influence outcomes, and success means doing better than rivals. Here we find the essence of strategic management.

Business executives aren't like shoppers picking a product or investors choosing a stock, simply making a choice that leads to one outcome or another. By the way they lead and communicate, and through their ability to inspire and encourage, executives can influence outcomes. That's the definition of "management." Moreover, they are in charge of organizations that compete vigorously with others; doing better than rivals is vital. That's where strategy comes in.

The decisions to enter a new market, release a new product, or acquire another firm are all in the fourth field, but we can find many examples beyond business. In sports, a coach shapes the performance of athletes, melding them into an effective team that can outperform the opponent. Or think of politics. For a voter, casting a ballot is essentially a first-field decision: You vote for the candidate you prefer. For the candidate, however, the reality is very different. Election day is the last hurdle in a

First-Field Research, Fourth-Field Decisions

In many of the most consequential decisions executives face—whether to acquire a company, say, or launch a new product—they can influence the outcomes, and their choices are successful only if they're better than the competition's.

These decisions fall into the fourth field of a matrix that categorizes decisions along two dimensions: our control over the outcome and whether the outcome depends on other people's decisions. We would benefit greatly from improving how we make these fourth-field decisions. Yet most recent research has examined judgment and choice in first-field decisions, which offer no control over outcomes and can be successful regardless of what anyone else does.

This focus stems in part from the power of carefully controlled experiments, which are an ideal way to isolate the cognitive mechanisms of human thought. By asking subjects to make choices among clearly stated options or to make judgments about things they cannot influence, we derive responses that can be neatly compared, free of extraneous factors. Decision research has made profound contributions because of the rigor of its experimental methods.

The unintentional effect, however, is that less research has focused on the second and third fields, and much less on the fourth field, where the ability to influence outcomes makes the comparison of responses across people problematic, and where the need to outperform rivals adds further complexity. Thus the paradox: Fourth-field decisions, which in real life include many of the most important, have received the least attention.

Decision experiments have certainly improved our understanding of the human mind, with many practical applications. The danger lies in taking the findings that are appropriate for one kind of decision and applying them to other kinds. We should not be surprised if business executives seem not to embrace this advice. Strategic decisions are fundamentally different from the routine choices and judgments so elegantly captured in laboratory settings. To do justice to the decisions executives face, researchers should employ a wider range of methods.

long process in which performance is relative—only one person can win—and outcomes can and must be shaped. Candidates need to inspire donors, build an organization, attract and motivate campaign workers, and ultimately persuade voters. A winning political campaign depends on a smart assessment of rivals as well as the ability to mobilize supporters, often in the face of long odds.

The fourth field includes some of the most consequential decisions of all, but because of their complexity they don't lend themselves to the careful controls of laboratory experiments, so we know less about how best to make them. (See the sidebar "First-Field Research, Fourth-Field Decisions.") What sort of mindset do they require? When we can influence outcomes, it is useful to summon high levels of self-belief. And when we need to outperform rivals, such elevated levels are not just useful but indeed essential. Only those who are able to muster a degree of commitment and determination that is by some definitions excessive will be in a position to win. That's not to say that wildly optimistic thinking will predictably lead to success. It won't. But in tough competitive situations where positive thinking can influence outcomes, only those who are willing to go beyond what seems reasonable will succeed.

In recent years a great deal of attention has focused on teaching executives to be aware of common biases and to avoid their ill effects. (See "Before You Make That Big Decision . . ." by Daniel Kahneman, Dan Lovallo, and Olivier Sibony, HBR, June 2011.) Of course it's good to appreciate the lessons of cognitive psychology and to understand the propensity for common errors. But if we apply those lessons to the world of strategic management, we're missing a trick. When facing decisions in the fourth field, executives need on the one hand a talent for careful and dispassionate analysis, which we call left-brain thinking, and on the other hand a willingness to push boundaries, which we call the right stuff.

Discernment and Versatility

In the course of their daily responsibilities, executives face a range of decisions, often in each of the four fields outlined here. Before making any decision, the most important thing is to understand which field it is in. For routine judgments and choices, where we cannot influence outcomes and need not consider the competition, well-known lessons about avoiding common biases make good sense. For other decisions, a different set of skills is needed.

In his profile of St. Louis Cardinals manager Tony La Russa, Buzz Bissinger wrote that baseball managers require "the combination of skills essential to the trade: part tactician, part psychologist, part riverboat gambler." That's a good description of many kinds of decision makers, in business as well as in sports. The tactician plays a competitive game—sensing the actions of rivals, anticipating the way a given move may lead to a countermove, and planning the best response. The psychologist must shape outcomes by inspiring others, by setting goals and providing encouragement, and by offering clear and direct feedback. The riverboat gambler knows that outcomes aren't just a matter of cold numbers and probabilities; it's also important to read an opponent in order to know when to raise the stakes, when to bluff, and when to fold.

Decision makers need to develop two vital skills. First, they must be able to discern the nature of the decision at hand. Second, they need to respond with the appropriate approach, able to act now as a psychologist, then as a tactician, next as a riverboat gambler, and perhaps once again as a psychologist. When it comes to the most complex decisions of all, those that drive the fortunes of organizations, executives need more than an ability to avoid common errors. They require a seemingly contradictory blend: a talent for clear-eyed analysis and the ability to take bold action.

Originally published in November 2013. Reprint R1311F

5

Noise

How to Overcome the High, Hidden
Cost of Inconsistent Decision Making

by Daniel Kahneman, Andrew M. Rosenfield, Linnea Gandhi, and Tom Blaser

A t a global financial services firm we worked with, a longtime customer accidentally submitted the same application file to two offices. Though the employees who reviewed the file were supposed to follow the same guidelines—and thus arrive at similar outcomes—the separate offices returned very different quotes. Taken aback, the customer gave the business to a competitor. From the point of view of the firm, employees in the same role should have been interchangeable, but in this case they were not. Unfortunately, this is a common problem.

Professionals in many organizations are assigned arbitrarily to cases: appraisers in credit-rating agencies, physicians in emergency rooms, underwriters of loans and insurance, and others.

Organizations expect consistency from these professionals: Identical cases should be treated similarly, if not identically. The problem is that humans are unreliable decision makers; their judgments are strongly influenced by irrelevant factors, such as their current mood, the time since their last meal, and the weather. We call the chance variability of judgments *noise*. It is an invisible tax on the bottom line of many companies.

Some jobs are noise-free. Clerks at a bank or a post office perform complex tasks, but they must follow strict rules that limit subjective judgment and guarantee, by design, that identical cases will be treated identically. In contrast, medical professionals, loan officers, project managers, judges, and executives all make judgment calls, which are guided by informal experience and general principles rather than by rigid rules. And if they don't reach precisely the same answer that every other person in their role would, that's acceptable; this is what we mean when we say that a decision is "a matter of judgment." A firm whose employees exercise judgment does not expect decisions to be entirely free of noise. But often noise is *far above* the level that executives would consider tolerable—and they are completely unaware of it.

The prevalence of noise has been demonstrated in several studies. Academic researchers have repeatedly confirmed that professionals often contradict their own prior judgments when given the same data on different occasions. For instance, when software developers were asked on two separate days to estimate the completion time for a given task, the hours they projected differed by 71%, on average. When pathologists made two assessments of the severity of biopsy results, the correlation between their ratings was only .61 (out of a perfect 1.0), indicating that they made inconsistent diagnoses quite frequently. Judgments made by different people are even more likely to diverge.

Idea in Brief

The Problem

Many organizations expect consistency from their professional employees. However, human judgment is often influenced by such irrelevant factors as the weather and the last case seen. More important, decisions often vary from employee to employee. The chance variability of judgments is called *noise,* and it is surprisingly costly to companies.

The Starting Point

Managers should perform a noise audit in which members of a unit, working independently, evaluate a common set of cases. The degree to which their decisions vary is the measure of noise. It will often be dramatically higher than executives anticipate.

The Solution

The most radical solution to a severe noise problem is to replace human judgment with algorithms. Algorithms are not difficult to construct—but often they're politically or operationally infeasible. In such instances, companies should establish procedures to help professionals achieve greater consistency.

Research has confirmed that in many tasks, experts' decisions are highly variable: valuing stocks, appraising real estate, sentencing criminals, evaluating job performance, auditing financial statements, and more. The unavoidable conclusion is that professionals often make decisions that deviate significantly from those of their peers, from their own prior decisions, and from rules that they themselves claim to follow.

Noise is often insidious: It causes even successful companies to lose substantial amounts of money without realizing it. How substantial? To get an estimate, we asked executives in one of the organizations we studied the following: "Suppose the optimal assessment of a case is $100,000. What would be the cost to the organization if the professional in charge of the case assessed a value of $115,000? What would be the cost of assessing it at $85,000?" The cost estimates were high. Aggregated over the assessments made every year, the cost of noise was measured in billions—an unacceptable number even for a large global firm. The value of reducing noise even by a few percentage points would be in the tens of millions. Remarkably, the organization had completely ignored the question of consistency until then.

It has long been known that predictions and decisions generated by simple statistical algorithms are often more accurate than those made by experts, even when the experts have access to more information than the formulas use. It is less well known that the key advantage of algorithms is that they are noise-free: Unlike humans, a formula will always return the same output for any given input. Superior consistency allows even simple and imperfect algorithms to achieve greater accuracy than human professionals. (Of course, there are times when algorithms will be operationally or politically infeasible, as we will discuss.)

In this article we explain the difference between noise and bias and look at how executives can audit the level and impact of noise in their organizations. We then describe an inexpensive, underused method for building algorithms that remediate noise, and we sketch out procedures that can promote consistency when algorithms are not an option.

Noise Versus Bias

When people consider errors in judgment and decision making, they most likely think of social biases like the stereotyping of minorities or of cognitive biases such as overconfidence and unfounded optimism. The useless variability that we call noise is a different type of error. To appreciate the distinction, think of your bathroom scale. We would say that the scale is *biased* if its readings are generally either too high or too low. If your weight appears to depend on where you happen to place your feet, the scale is *noisy*. A scale that consistently underestimates true weight by exactly four pounds is seriously biased but free of noise. A scale that gives two different readings when you step on it twice is noisy. Many errors of measurement arise from a combination of bias and noise. Most inexpensive bathroom scales are somewhat biased and quite noisy.

For a visual illustration of the distinction, consider the targets in the exhibit "How noise and bias affect accuracy." These show the results of target practice for four-person teams in which each individual shoots once.

- Team A is *accurate*: The shots of the teammates are on the bull's-eye and close to one another.

The other three teams are inaccurate but in distinctive ways:

- Team B is *noisy*: The shots of its members are centered around the bull's-eye but widely scattered.

- Team C is *biased*: The shots all missed the bull's-eye but cluster together.

- Team D is both *noisy* and *biased*.

As a comparison of teams A and B illustrates, an increase in noise always impairs accuracy when there is no bias. When bias is present, increasing noise may actually cause a lucky hit, as happened for team D. Of course, no organization would put its trust in luck. Noise is always undesirable—and sometimes disastrous.

How noise and bias affect accuracy

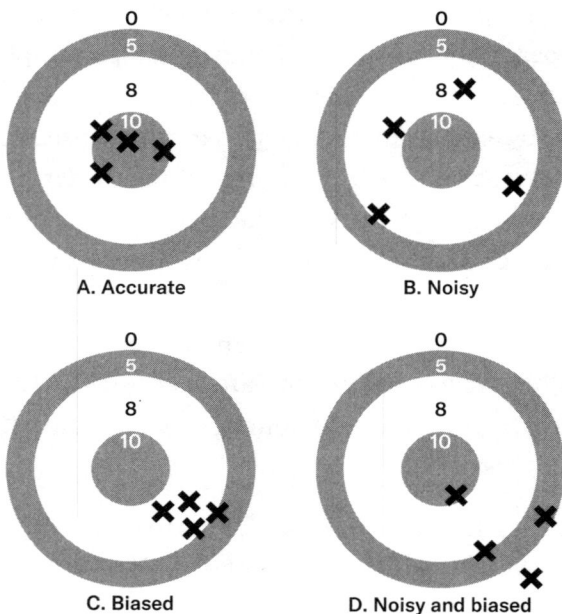

A. Accurate

B. Noisy

C. Biased

D. Noisy and biased

It is obviously useful to an organization to know about bias and noise in the decisions of its employees, but collecting that information isn't straightforward. Different issues arise in measuring these errors. A major problem is that the outcomes of decisions often aren't known until far in the future, if at all. Loan officers, for example, frequently must wait several years to see how loans they approved worked out, and they almost never know what happens to an applicant they reject.

Unlike bias, noise can be measured without knowing what an accurate response would be. To illustrate, imagine that the targets at which the shooters aimed were erased from the exhibit. You would know nothing about the teams' overall accuracy, but you could be certain that something was wrong with the scattered shots of teams B and D: Wherever the bull's-eye was, they did not all come close to hitting it. All that's required to measure noise in judgments is a simple experiment in which a few realistic cases are evaluated independently by several professionals. Here again, the scattering of judgments can be observed without knowing the correct answer. We call such experiments *noise audits*.

Performing a Noise Audit

The point of a noise audit is not to produce a report. The ultimate goal is to improve the quality of decisions, and an audit can be successful only if the leaders of the unit are prepared to accept unpleasant results and act on them. Such buy-in is easier to achieve if the executives view the study as their own creation. To that end, the cases should be compiled by respected team members and should cover the range of problems typically encountered. To make the results relevant to everyone, all unit members should participate in the audit. A social scientist with experience in conducting rigorous behavioral experiments should supervise the technical aspects of the audit, but the professional unit must own the process.

Recently, we helped two financial services organizations conduct noise audits. The duties and expertise of the two groups we studied were quite different, but both required the evaluation of moderately complex materials and often involved decisions about hundreds of thousands of dollars. We followed the same protocol in both organizations. First we asked managers of the professional teams involved to construct several realistic case files for evaluation. To prevent information about the experiment from leaking, the entire exercise was conducted on the same day. Employees were asked to spend about half the day analyzing two to four cases. They were to decide on a dollar amount for each, as in their normal routine. To avoid collusion, the participants were not told that the study was concerned with reliability. In one organization, for example, the goals were described as understanding the employees' professional thinking, increasing their tools' usefulness, and improving communication among colleagues. About 70 professionals in organization A participated, and about 50 in organization B.

We constructed a noise index for each case, which answered the following question: "By how much do the judgments of two randomly chosen employees differ?" We expressed this amount as a percentage of their average. Suppose the assessments of a case by two employees are $600 and $1,000. The average of their assessments is $800, and the difference between them is $400, so the noise index is 50% for this pair. We performed the same computation for all pairs of employees and then calculated an overall average noise index for each case.

Pre-audit interviews with executives in the two organizations indicated that they expected the differences between their professionals' decisions to range from 5% to 10%—a level they considered acceptable for "matters of judgment." The results came as a shock. The noise index ranged from 34% to 62% for the six cases in organization A, and the overall average was 48%. In the four cases in organization B, the noise index ranged from 46% to 70%, with an average of 60%. Perhaps most disappointing, experience on the job did not appear to reduce noise. Among professionals with five or more years on the job, average disagreement was 46% in organization A and 62% in organization B.

No one had seen this coming. But because they owned the study, the executives in both organizations accepted the conclusion that the judgments of their professionals were unreliable to an extent that could not be tolerated. All quickly agreed that something had to be done to control the problem.

Because the findings were consistent with prior research on the low reliability of professional judgment, they didn't surprise us. The major puzzle for us was the fact that neither organization had ever considered reliability to be an issue.

The problem of noise is effectively invisible in the business world; we have observed that audiences are quite surprised when the reliability of professional judgment is mentioned as an issue. What prevents companies from recognizing that the judgments of their employees are noisy? The answer lies in two familiar phenomena: Experienced professionals tend to have high confidence in the accuracy of their own judgments, and they also have high regard for their colleagues' intelligence. This combination inevitably leads to an overestimation of agreement. When asked about what their colleagues would say, professionals expect others' judgments to be much closer to their own than they actually are. Most of the time, of course, experienced professionals are completely unconcerned with what others might think and simply assume that theirs is the best answer. One reason the problem of noise is invisible is that people do not go through life imagining plausible alternatives to every judgment they make.

The expectation that others will agree with you is sometimes justified, particularly where judgments are so skilled that they are intuitive. High-level chess and driving are standard examples of tasks that have been practiced to near perfection. Master players who look at a situation on a chessboard will all have very similar assessments of the state of the game—whether, say, the white queen is in danger or black's king-side defense is weak. The same is true of drivers. Negotiating traffic would be impossibly dangerous if we could not assume that the drivers around us share our understanding of priorities at intersections and roundabouts. There is little or no noise at high levels of skill.

High skill develops in chess and driving through years of practice in a predictable environment, in which actions are followed by feedback that is both immediate and clear. Unfortunately, few professionals operate in such a world. In most jobs people learn to make judgments by hearing managers and colleagues explain and criticize—a much less reliable source of knowledge than learning from one's mistakes. Long experience on a job always increases people's confidence in their judgments, but in the absence of rapid feedback, confidence is no guarantee of either accuracy or consensus.

We offer this aphorism in summary: *Where there is judgment, there is noise—and usually more of it than you think.* As a rule, we believe that neither professionals nor their managers can make a good guess about the reliability of their judgments. The only way to get an accurate assessment is to conduct a noise audit. And at least in some cases, the problem will be severe enough to require action.

Dialing Down the Noise

The most radical solution to the noise problem is to replace human judgment with formal rules—known as algorithms—that use the data about a case to produce a prediction or a decision. People have competed against algorithms in several hundred contests of accuracy over the past 60 years, in tasks ranging from predicting the life expectancy of cancer patients

Types of noise and bias

Bias and noise are distinct kinds of error. Each comes in different variants and requires different corrective actions.

Type of bias	Examples	Corrective actions
General The average judgment is wrong.	• Planning fallacy: Forecasts of outcomes are mostly optimistic • Excessive risk aversion: A venture capital firm rejects too many promising but risky investments	• Continual monitoring of decisions • Guidelines and targets for the frequency of certain outcomes (such as loan approvals) • Eliminating incentives that favor biases
Social Discrimination occurs against—or for—certain categories of cases.	• Frequent denial of credit to qualified applicants from certain ethnic groups • Gender bias in assessments of job performance	• Monitoring statistics for different groups • Blinding of applications • Objective and quantifiable metrics • Open channels for complaints • Guidelines and training
Cognitive Decisions are strongly influenced by irrelevant factors or insensitive to relevant ones.	• Excessive effects of first impressions • Effects of anchors (such as an opening offer in negotiation) • Myopic neglect of future consequences	• Training employees to detect situations in which biases are likely to occur • Critiques of important decisions, focused on likely biases

Type of noise	Examples	Corrective actions
Variability across occasions Decisions vary when the same case is presented more than once to the same individual.	• A hiring officer's judgments of a file are influenced by her mood or the quality of the previous applicant	• Algorithms to replace human judgment • Checklists that encourage a consistent approach to decisions
Variability across individuals Professionals in the same role make different decisions.	• Some individuals are generally more lenient than others • Some individuals are more cautious than others	• Algorithms to replace human judgment • Frequent monitoring of individuals' decisions • Roundtables at which differences are explored and resolved • Checklists that encourage a consistent approach to decisions

to predicting the success of graduate students. Algorithms were more accurate than human professionals in about half the studies, and approximately tied with the humans in the others. The ties should also count as victories for the algorithms, which are more cost-effective.

In many situations, of course, algorithms will not be practical. The application of a rule may not be feasible when inputs are idiosyncratic or hard to code in a consistent format. Algorithms are also less likely to be useful for judgments or decisions that involve multiple dimensions or depend on negotiation with another party. Even when an algorithmic solution is available in principle, organizational considerations sometimes prevent implementation. The replacement of existing employees by software is a painful process that will encounter resistance unless it frees those employees up for more-enjoyable tasks.

But if the conditions are right, developing and implementing algorithms can be surprisingly easy. The common assumption is that algorithms require statistical analysis of large amounts of data. For example, most people we talk to believe that data on thousands of loan applications and their outcomes is needed to develop an equation that predicts commercial loan defaults. Very few know that adequate algorithms can be developed without any outcome data at all—and with input information on only a small number of cases. We call predictive formulas that are built without outcome data "reasoned rules," because they draw on commonsense reasoning.

The construction of a reasoned rule starts with the selection of a few (perhaps six to eight) variables that are incontrovertibly related to the outcome being predicted. If the outcome is loan default, for example, assets and liabilities will surely be included in the list. The next step is to assign these variables equal weight in the prediction formula, setting their sign in the obvious direction (positive for assets, negative for liabilities). The rule can then be constructed by a few simple calculations. (For more details, see the sidebar "How to Build a Reasoned Rule.")

The surprising result of much research is that in many contexts reasoned rules are about as accurate as statistical models built with outcome data. Standard statistical models combine a set of predictive variables, which are assigned weights based on their relationship to the predicted outcomes and to one another. In many situations, however, these weights are both statistically unstable and practically unimportant. A simple rule that assigns equal weights to the selected variables is likely to be just as valid. Algorithms that weight variables equally and don't rely on outcome data have proved successful in personnel selection, election forecasting, predictions about football games, and other applications.

The bottom line here is that if you plan to use an algorithm to reduce noise, you need not wait for outcome data. You can reap most of the benefits by using common sense to select variables and the simplest possible rule to combine them.

Of course, no matter what type of algorithm is employed, people must retain ultimate control. Algorithms must be monitored and adjusted for occasional changes in the population of cases. Managers must also keep an eye on individual decisions and have the authority to override the algorithm in clear-cut cases. For example, a decision to approve a loan should be provisionally reversed if the firm discovers that the applicant has been arrested. Most important, executives should determine how to translate the algorithm's output into action. The algorithm can tell you which prospective loans are in the top 5% or in the bottom 10% of all applications, but someone must decide what to do with that information.

How to Build a Reasoned Rule

You don't need outcome data to create useful predictive algorithms. For example, you can build a reasoned rule that predicts loan defaults quite effectively without knowing what happened to past loans; all you need is a small set of recent loan applications. Here are the next steps:

1. Select six to eight variables that are distinct and obviously related to the predicted outcome. Assets and revenues (weighted positively) and liabilities (weighted negatively) would surely be included, along with a few other features of loan applications.

2. Take the data from your set of cases (all the loan applications from the past year) and compute the mean and standard deviation of each variable in that set.

3. For every case in the set, compute a "standard score" for each variable: the difference between the value in the case and the mean of the whole set, divided by the standard deviation. With standard scores, all variables are expressed on the same scale and can be compared and averaged.

4. Compute a "summary score" for each case—the average of its variables' standard scores. This is the output of the reasoned rule. The same formula will be used for new cases, using the mean and standard deviation of the original set and updating periodically.

5. Order the cases in the set from high to low summary scores, and determine the appropriate actions for different ranges of scores. With loan applications, for instance, the actions might be "the top 10% of applicants will receive a discount" and "the bottom 30% will be turned down."

You are now ready to apply the rule to new cases. The algorithm will compute a summary score for each new case and generate a decision.

Algorithms are sometimes used as an intermediate source of information for professionals, who make the final decisions. One example is the Public Safety Assessment, a formula that was developed to help U.S. judges decide whether a defendant can be safely released pending trial. In its first six months of use in Kentucky, crime among defendants on pretrial release fell by about 15%, while the percentage of people released pretrial increased. It's obvious in this case that human judges must retain the final authority for the decisions: The public would be shocked to see justice meted out by a formula.

Uncomfortable as people may be with the idea, studies have shown that while humans can provide useful input to formulas, algorithms do better in the role of final decision maker. If the avoidance of errors is the only criterion, managers should be strongly advised to overrule the algorithm only in exceptional circumstances.

Bringing Discipline to Judgment

Replacing human decisions with an algorithm should be considered whenever professional judgments are noisy, but in most cases this solution will be too radical or simply impractical. An alternative is to adopt procedures that promote consistency by ensuring that employees in the same role use similar methods to seek information, integrate it into a view of the case, and translate that view into a decision. A thorough examination of everything required to do that is beyond the scope of this article, but we can offer some basic advice, with the important caveat that instilling discipline in judgment is not at all easy.

Training is crucial, of course, but even professionals who were trained together tend to drift into their own way of doing things.

Firms sometimes combat drift by organizing roundtables at which decision makers gather to review cases. Unfortunately, most roundtables are run in a way that makes it much too easy to achieve agreement, because participants quickly converge on the opinions stated first or most confidently. To prevent such spurious agreement, the individual participants in a roundtable should study the case independently, form opinions they're prepared to defend, and send those opinions to the group leader before the meeting. Such roundtables will effectively provide an audit of noise, with the added step of a group discussion in which differences of opinion are explored.

As an alternative or addition to roundtables, professionals should be offered user-friendly tools, such as checklists and carefully formulated questions, to guide them as they collect information about a case, make intermediate judgments, and formulate a final decision. Unwanted variability occurs at each of those stages, and firms can—and should—test how much such tools reduce it. Ideally, the people who use these tools will view them as aids that help them do their jobs effectively and economically. Unfortunately, our experience suggests that the task of constructing judgment tools that are both effective and user-friendly is more difficult than many executives think. Controlling noise is hard, but we expect that an organization that conducts an audit and evaluates the cost of noise in dollars will conclude that reducing random variability is worth the effort.

. . .

Our main goal in this article is to introduce managers to the concept of noise as a source of errors and explain how it is distinct from bias. The term *bias* has entered the public consciousness to the extent that the words *error* and *bias* are often used interchangeably. In fact, better decisions are not achieved merely by reducing general biases (such as optimism) or specific social and cognitive biases (such as discrimination against women or anchoring effects). Executives who are concerned with accuracy should also confront the prevalence of inconsistency in professional judgments. Noise is more difficult to appreciate than bias, but it is no less real or less costly.

Originally published in October 2016. Reprint R1610B

The Value of Human Decision-Making in the Age of AI

by Martin Reeves, Mihnea Moldoveanu, and Adam Job

The rapid advancement of AI has ignited enthusiasm about its potential to revolutionize corporate decision-making by substituting this technology for expensive, fallible humans. But it's naive to believe that by gathering ever more data and feeding it to ever more powerful algorithms alone, businesses can uncover the truth, make the right decisions, and create value. We call this false belief *dataism*.

Decisions are not merely exercises in data aggregation and algorithmic analysis. They necessarily involve many additional nuanced elements, such as selecting trustworthy data sources, employing imagination to envision possibilities beyond the available facts, and judging the feasibility of solutions. These are areas where humans have innate advantages over machines.

Crucially, they involve implicit and often-untrained human capabilities.

Consider the case of Kodak and Fuji. Both companies had access to the same data indicating the rise of digital photography, and they evaluated it in light of the same objectives of maximizing growth and profitability. Still, they came to different decisions: Kodak doubled down on its analog products, while Fuji diversified, investing in digital technologies and pursuing other options like cosmetics, which collectively were sufficient to ensure its survival. The same data inspired yet another decision for Sony, which, as a challenger in the market, saw the rise in digital photography as an opportunity worth embracing.

This divergence underscores that decisions depend on interpretation, context, and strategic framing—areas where human judgment will remain essential.

A Holistic View of Decision-Making

In light of our experience with corporate decision-making, as well as the literature on decision science (for example, from the military, health care, and R&D), we have identified eight dimensions that, beyond data and algorithms, factor into most decisions, albeit often implicitly. They can be understood through the simple example of purchasing a car.

1. Defining the ultimate goal

Every decision ultimately serves a human end. Specifying that end is key to understanding what success might look like. The human end for a car buyer might be signaling their status with a luxury vehicle or ensuring their children have a safe way to travel to and from school.

Idea in Brief

The Challenge

As AI systems become more capable, many organizations are tempted to offload complex decisions to them. But overreliance on AI can lead to blind spots, ethical oversights, and a loss of human judgment in moments that demand it most.

The Solution

Rather than replacing human judgment, organizations should design decision-making processes that combine it with AI. This means clearly defining when and how AI tools should inform decisions—and when values, experience, and ethical reasoning must take the lead. Human decision-making remains irreplaceable when we are navigating ambiguity, weighing competing values, and understanding the broader impact of choices.

The Implications

Leaders who strike the right balance between AI and human judgment—preserving what each does best—can make smarter, more responsible decisions.

Businesses too have ultimate goals—from achieving economic prosperity to contributing to society to protecting the environment—which can differ markedly. Given the subjectivity of human values, defining the human end cannot be outsourced to machine intelligence.

2. Framing the immediate objectives

To achieve your ultimate goal, you often have to make smaller, more immediate, and tangible decisions along the way. In our car-buying example, the ultimate goal may be to purchase a vehicle that meets certain safety standards, but you also want to make sure that the car fits within a given budget. For a business, the ultimate goal might be to achieve 10% sales growth over the previous year, but you also have to ensure that optimizing short-term sales growth doesn't compromise long-term brand reputation.

This kind of decision framing cannot be derived from data and analytic tools alone, since it involves trading off individual and collective preferences. Human involvement is paramount in identifying these objectives and balancing them. Quite often, they need to be refined through iterative interactions, as humans often discover what they really want by pursuing an objective and adjusting as they discover new features and new sources of value.

3. Charting the realm of the possible

Once the objectives are defined, it's time to identify possible options. While data is important input for this step, it will not usually tell the full story. Data is retrospective, but human decisions are often based on counterfactuals: what *might* happen and how we could influence the likelihood of different possibilities playing out.

Human imagination extends the realm of the possible. For example, if a car buyer needs a short commute to work, they might consider alternatives like public transportation, ride-sharing services, or electric scooters.

All firms are built on an act of imagination. For instance, Airbnb's founders envisioned a platform where homeowners could rent out spare rooms—upending the belief of leading hospitality companies that you had to build or own the accommodations offered to customers. This idea didn't emerge from an analysis of existing hospitality data but came from humans imagining how they could address the need for affordable lodging.

4. Selecting data sources

Assessing your options can benefit from relevant data. But even though the word *data* derives from the Latin *datum* (something that is given), data needs to be created: captured, filtered, selected, interpreted, and corrected—a task that requires human agency and discernment.

We must avoid the trap of focusing only on given or easily accessible data. In our car-purchasing scenario, relying solely on manufacturer-provided fuel-efficiency data may not provide the complete picture. Supplementing this with independent reviews of real-world performance can lead to a more informed decision.

In business, think of the ease with which we can query current customers on their satisfaction with our offerings—and of the additional insights gained speaking to noncustomers about why they are choosing a competitor's services or not choosing any service at all.

Moreover, not all valuable information is quantifiable. For a car, factors like comfort, aesthetics, or driving experience are subjective. We need to identify proxies for these qualitative aspects or gather firsthand experience to fill in the gaps. For example, Procter & Gamble developed the Swiffer after ethnographic studies (observations of consumers in their homes) identified a desire for more-convenient cleaning methods— information that could not be gleaned from existing quantitative datasets.

5. Establishing trustworthiness

In an era where misinformation can spread rapidly, establishing the credibility of data sources is more critical than ever.

AI systems lack this ability. Humans, on the other hand, can evaluate the reputation, expertise, and potential incentives or biases of information providers.

For example, in the car-buying process, a buyer might trust recommendations from friends or family over advertisements from manufacturers. In business, assessing the incentives and credibility of different data sources ensures that decisions are based on reliable information.

6. Choosing a decision algorithm

While many AI products are marketed as being universally useful, mathematics has shown that no single optimization algorithm can be superior across all problems. Thus, humans must decide which decision-making framework aligns best with their objectives.

In the car example, a cost-focused buyer might use a tool that calculates life-cycle-ownership costs, while another buyer who prioritizes aesthetics might choose a very different approach. One buyer may forgo the expected value of perfect computation and opt for a fast and frugal set of heuristics, and another may prefer an exhaustive search process.

7. Assessing competitiveness

When purchasing a car, solving the functional problem—namely, choosing a practical option that satisfies your objectives—may be sufficient, unless, of course, you are competing for status with your neighbors or classmates. In business, the ideal solution usually needs to be competitively advantageous by being clearly better than competitors' likely responses and hard for others to imitate. Solving the same problems your competitors face by using the same data and algorithms they have access to will not reveal unique or superior opportunities. Rather, it is tantamount to commoditizing your business by using a generic problem-solving process.

Human strategists play a vital role in assessing the competitive implications of decisions by understanding the incentives, advantages, mindsets, and behavioral patterns of competitors. For example, Apple's success with the iPhone was driven not merely by incorporating the most advanced technology but also by emphasizing design aesthetics, user experience, and ecosystem integration.

8. Incorporating ethical considerations

The functionally, economically, or competitively superior solution may not be ethically acceptable. Humans are responsible for ensuring that decisions adhere to ethical norms and societal values. This requires the application of models and principles of moral reasoning to the specific interpersonal and social context of the decision—which is also a quintessentially human ability.

In the car-purchase example, a buyer might consider the environmental impact of their choice, opting for an electric vehicle over a gasoline-powered one, even if it costs more.

New Rules for Human-Led, AI-Supported Decision-Making

Many crucial aspects of decision-making lie beyond the realms of data and algorithms. Indeed, the spread of more-powerful tools and larger datasets will likely make the human elements of decision-making more differentiating.

However, human capabilities like moral judgments, imagination, and intuition are often untrained, impulsive, or implicit.

Thus, to distinguish and elevate their decision-making processes, organizations need to actively codify and foster the requisite human decision-making skills. We outline five imperatives toward this end.

Reject simplistic dataism

Leaders should acknowledge that effective decision-making encompasses more than data analysis and algorithmic optimization. This does not mean abandoning AI tools and techniques—it means integrating AI in a more holistic, human-led process. The emerging discipline of designing and deploying bespoke AI agents, jointly shaped by human acts of interpretation and imagination and by the computational and informational resources of large language models, offers one path forward.

Ensure that problem-solvers get their hands dirty

Just as pilots practice manual flying to keep their skills sharp despite the availability of autopilot systems, business leaders should immerse themselves in the underlying phenomena of their industries to prevent overreliance on AI and to maintain critical decision-making skills. This entails direct engagement with customers, employees, competitors, and regulators.

For example, Toyota's *genchi genbutsu* philosophy, meaning "go and see for yourself," encourages managers to visit the shop floor to observe processes firsthand. This practice helps identify inefficiencies and fosters a deeper understanding that data alone cannot provide.

Make implicit human decision-making skills explicit

Human decisions are often shaped by intuition—our powerful, unconscious intelligence that's based on our experience and heuristics. Companies can help employees develop their intuition through acknowledging and fostering experiential learning and having decision-maker participants reflect on questions like these:

- What was my initial reaction or gut feeling?

- Where did I rely on individual or collective experience?

- Where did I supplement my experience or expertise?

- What mental shortcuts did I rely on to simplify the decision?

Another uniquely human skill is imagination—the ability to come up with what does not yet exist, but could. While imagination is often believed to be the result of uncontrollable strokes of genius, organizations can actually systematically harness imagination through tactics like seeking out anomalies (rather than focusing on averages), questioning previously held assumptions, and conducting experiments.

Foster an environment where human skills can thrive

It may be difficult for intuition and imagination to shine in a technocratic culture dominated by rational justification. To create an environment that promotes unique human decision-making skills, organizations must begin with a culture of psychological safety in which employees can express diverse perspectives, debate ideas openly, and challenge the status quo.

Build hybrid decision-making systems

With human skills appropriately honed, leaders must set about rebuilding decision-making systems that combine the best of human and AI capabilities.

This approach may involve segmenting decision-making tasks best suited for AI—such as data processing, pattern recognition, and optimization for quantifiable criteria—from those requiring human judgment, like setting objectives and considering ethics, values, and context.

The pumpkin spice latte, one of Starbucks' most successful products, is an example of human decision-makers taking the lead and leveraging their understanding of context. While initial tests showed that customers preferred the taste of chocolate or caramel-flavored products, the product developers believed that for a seasonal special, uniqueness was even more important than taste. In subsequent studies, they gathered information on this criterion, where the pumpkin flavor excelled.

There will also be tasks where human intelligence and machine intelligence intersect and cooperate, forming what might be called a bionic organization in which humans review AI-generated solutions to assess their feasibility as well as their ethical and competitive implications. Consider Netflix, which is famous for basing production choices on its vast trove of viewership data. Its decision to create the chart-topping show *Stranger Things* may have been driven by an observation that content dealing with supernatural themes performed well or by the enduring popularity of 1980s shows. However, Netflix also had to make several bets driven by intuition, such as hiring a pair of unproven showrunners who would inject their own vision or taking a chance on a set of inexperienced child actors.

· · ·

As AI grows ever more capable, the belief—or fear—that it can substitute for human decision-making grows more prevalent.

However, decisions entail more than data collection and analysis, and humans have innate advantages over even the most powerful AI in these domains. Thus, the rise of AI presents an opportunity for us to step up to the challenge of refining, emphasizing, and applying our own human strengths to differentiate corporate decision-making.

Adapted from "The Irreplaceable Value of Human Decision-Making in the Age of AI" on hbr.org, December 11, 2024. Reprint H08IKZ

6

Where Data-Driven Decision-Making Can Go Wrong

by Michael Luca and Amy C. Edmondson

L et's say you're leading a meeting about the hourly pay of your company's warehouse employees. For several years it has automatically been increased by small amounts to keep up with inflation. Citing a study of a large company that found that higher pay improved productivity so much that it boosted profits, someone on your team advocates for a different approach: a substantial raise of $2 an hour for all workers in the warehouse. What would you do?

Too often business leaders go in one of two directions in these moments: either taking the evidence presented as gospel or dismissing it altogether. Both approaches are misguided. Leaders instead should organize discussions that thoughtfully evaluate seemingly relevant evidence and its applicability to a given situation.

In the scenario just described you should pose a series of questions aimed at assessing the potential impact of wage increases on your company specifically. You might ask:

- Can you tell us more about the setting of the research to help us evaluate whether it applies to our warehouse employees?

- How do our wages stack up against those of other employers competing for our workers, and how does that compare with the study?

- Was an experiment conducted? If not, what approach was used to understand whether higher wages were driving the productivity change or simply reflecting it?

- What measures of productivity were used, and how long were the effects measured?

- What other analyses or data might be relevant?

Of course, tone matters. These questions must be asked in a genuine spirit of curiosity, with a desire to learn and get sound recommendations.

Whether evidence comes from an outside study or internal data, walking through it thoroughly before making major decisions is crucial. In our interactions with companies—including data-heavy tech firms—we've noticed that this practice isn't consistently followed. Too often predetermined beliefs, problematic comparisons, and groupthink dominate discussions. Research from psychology and economics suggests that biases—such as *base rate neglect*, the tendency to overlook general statistical information in favor of specific case information or anecdotes, and *confirmation bias*, the propensity to seek out and

Idea in Brief

The Problem

When managers are presented with internal data or an external study, all too often they either automatically accept its accuracy and relevance to their business or dismiss it out of hand.

Why It Happens

Leaders mistakenly conflate causation with correlation, underestimate the importance of sample size, focus on the wrong outcomes, misjudge generalizability, or overweigh a specific result.

The Right Approach

Leaders should ask probing questions about the evidence in a rigorous discussion about its usefulness. They should create a psychologically safe environment so that participants will feel comfortable offering diverse points of view.

overweight results that support your existing beliefs—also hinder the systematic weighing of evidence. But companies don't have to fall into this pattern. Drawing on our research, work with companies, and teaching experience (including executive education classes in leadership and business analytics and a recent MBA course called Data-Driven Leadership), we have developed an approach general managers can apply to discussions of data so that they can make better decisions.

Pressure-Test the Link Between Cause and Effect

Will search engine advertisements increase sales? Will allowing employees to work remotely reduce turnover? These questions are about cause and effect—and are the kinds of questions that data analytics can help answer. In fact, research papers have looked at them in detail. However, managers frequently misinterpret how the findings of those and other studies apply to their own business situation. When making decisions, managers should consider *internal validity*—whether an analysis accurately answers a question in the context in which it was studied. They should also consider *external validity*—the extent to which they can generalize results from one context to another. That will help them avoid making five common mistakes:

Conflating causation with correlation

Even though most people know that correlation doesn't equal causation, this error is surprisingly prevalent. Take eBay's advertising strategy. For years the company had advertised on search engines such as Google, looking to grow demand by attracting more customers. A consulting report concluded that the ads were effective, noting that when more ads were shown in a market, the total value of purchases on eBay was higher. Alas, it had reached the wrong conclusion about those ads. With the help of an experiment conducted by a team of economists led by Steven Tadelis of the University of California Berkeley, eBay realized that the correlation was explained by advertisements targeting people already likely to visit eBay and markets where demand for eBay would be expected to spike even without ads.

To understand causality, delve into how the study in question was conducted. For instance, was it a *randomized controlled trial*, in which the researchers randomly assigned people to two groups: one that was subjected to a test condition and a control group that was not? That's often considered the gold standard for assessing cause and effect, though such experiments aren't always feasible or practical. Perhaps the researchers relied on a *natural experiment*, observing the effects of an event or a policy change on specific groups. For example, a study might examine

How to avoid predictable errors

Pressure-testing assumptions, especially before difficult-to-reverse decisions are made, is increasingly vital. Here are five common pitfalls leaders make in interpreting analyses, along with the questions that will help you steer clear of them.

To prevent this problem	Ask about this	Sample questions
Conflating correlation and causation	Approach to determining causality	Was this analysis based on an experiment? If not, are there confounders (variables that affect the independent and dependent variables)? To what extent were they addressed in the analysis?
Misjudging the potential magnitude of effects	Sample size and the precision of the results	What was the average effect of the change? What was the sample size and the confidence interval (or range of likely values the true effect would fall into, and the degree to which one is certain it would fall into that range)? How would our course of action change, depending on where the true effect might lie?
Making a disconnect between what is measured and what matters	Outcome measures	What outcomes were measured? Were they broad enough? Did they capture key intended and unintended consequences? Were they tracked for an appropriate period of time? Were all relevant outcomes reported? How do we think they map to broader organizational goals?
Misjudging generalizability	Empirical setting and subgroup analysis	How similar is the setting of this study to our business context? Does the context or time period of the analysis make it more or less relevant to our decision? What is the composition of the sample being studied, and how does it influence the applicability of the results? Does the effect vary across subgroups or settings? Does this tell us anything about the generalizability of the results?
Overweighting a specific result	Broader evidence and further data collection	Are there other analyses that validate the results and approach? What additional data could we collect, and would the benefit of gathering it outweigh the cost of collecting it? How might this change our interpretation of the results?

the impact of a benefit whose recipients were chosen by lottery, which allows researchers to compare how the benefit changed the circumstances or behavior of those who won the lottery with that of those who didn't win.

Researchers who don't have access to planned or natural experiments may instead control for potential confounding factors—variables that affect the variable of interest—in their data analysis, though this can be challenging in practice. For instance, if you were assessing the impact of a training program on productivity, you'd want to make sure you controlled for prior experience and other things that might affect productivity.

Underestimating the importance of sample size

Imagine two hospitals: a large one that handles thousands of births each year, and a small one with a few hundred births annually. Which hospital do you think would have more days where more than 60% of the babies born were boys?

The answer is the small hospital because it has more variability in daily birth numbers. Small sample sizes are more likely to show greater fluctuations. Psychologists Daniel Kahneman and Amos Tversky, in their canonical work on biases and heuristics, found that most people got the answer wrong, with more than half saying, "About the same." People tend to underappreciate the effect that sample size has on the precision of an estimate. This common error can lead to bad decisions. Whether you're trying to figure out how much to trust online reviews, how to interpret productivity trends, or how much weight to put on the results of an advertising experiment, the size of the sample being analyzed is important to consider.

When evaluating effects, it can be helpful to ask not only about the sample size but about the *confidence interval*. A confidence interval provides a range of values that the true effect is likely to fall into, and the degree to which one is certain it falls into that range. The answers should shape the conversation about which course of action you'll take.

Focusing on the wrong outcomes

In their classic 1992 HBR article "The Balanced Scorecard—Measures That Drive Performance," Robert S. Kaplan and David P. Norton opened with a simple observation: "What you measure is what you get." Although their article predates the era of modern analytics, that idea is more apt than ever. Experiments and predictive analytics often focus on outcomes that are easy to measure rather than on those that business leaders truly care about but are difficult or impractical to ascertain. As a result, outcome metrics often don't fully capture broader performance in company operations.

Let's return to the example of wage increases. Costs are easily measured, while boosts in productivity can be difficult to quantify. That can lead managers to focus narrowly on the cost of better pay and fail to appreciate the potential gains. A broader analysis would take an approach like the one seen in a study by economists Natalia Emanuel and Emma Harrington. They set out to understand the implications of warehouse pay levels set by a large online retailer. The researchers examined changes in productivity after a 2019 pay increase for warehouse workers and found that improvements in productivity and turnover were so large that the wage increases more than paid for themselves. They found similar results when they looked at the effects of higher pay on the productivity and turnover of customer service employees.

It's also important to make sure that the outcome being studied is a good proxy for the actual organizational goal in question. Some company experiments track results for just a few days and assume that they're robust evidence of what the longer-term effect would be. With certain questions and contexts, a short time frame may not be sufficient. One company that works to avoid this problem is Amazon: It invests heavily in exploring the longer-term costs and benefits of possible product changes. There are many ways to assess the relevance and interpretation of outcomes, ranging from clear discussions about limitations to formal analyses of the link between short-term effects and longer-term ones.

To really learn from any dataset, you need to ask basic questions like, What outcomes were measured, and did we include all that are relevant to the decision we have to make? Were they broad enough to capture key intended and unintended consequences? Were they tracked for an appropriate period of time?

Misjudging generalizability

With the example of the warehouse wage increase, a vital question is what the results from one set of warehouses imply for a different set. Moreover, a company may wish to know how the results apply to, say, restaurant or retail employees.

We have seen business leaders make missteps in both directions, either over- or underestimating the generalizability of findings. For instance, when the senior vice president of engineering at a major tech company told us about his company's rule against looking at university grades in engineer hiring decisions, we asked about the rationale. He said that Google had "proved that grades don't matter"—referring to a Google executive's comment he had read somewhere, claiming there wasn't a relationship between school grades and career outcomes. By taking that piece of information as gospel, he ignored potential limitations to both its internal and its external validity.

When you're assessing generalizability, it can be helpful to discuss the mechanisms that might explain the results and whether they apply in other contexts. You might ask things like, How similar is the setting of this study to that of our business? Does the context or period of the analysis make it more or less relevant to our decision? What is the composition of the sample being studied, and how does it influence the applicability of the results? Does the effect vary across subgroups?

Overweighting a specific result

Relying on a single empirical finding without a systematic discussion of it can be just as unwise as dismissing the evidence as irrelevant to your situation. It's worth checking for additional research on the subject. Conducting an experiment or further analysis with your own organization can be another good option. Questions to ask include, Are there other analyses that validate the results and the approach? What additional data might we collect, and would the benefit of gathering more evidence outweigh the cost of that effort?

Start by Speaking Up

In 1906, Sir Francis Galton famously analyzed data on a contest at a livestock fair in which people guessed the weight of an ox. Though individual guesses were all over the map, the average of the guesses was nearly spot-on—demonstrating the *wisdom of the crowd*. Harnessing that wisdom can be challenging, however. Collective intelligence is best when mechanisms are in place to promote active and diverse participation. Otherwise, crowds can also amplify bias—especially when they're homogeneous in viewpoint.

To overcome bias, business leaders can invite contributors with diverse perspectives to a conversation, ask them to challenge and build on ideas, and ensure that discussions are probing and draw on high-quality data. (See "What You Don't Know About Making Decisions," by David A. Garvin and Michael Roberto, HBR, September 2001.) Encouraging dissent and constructive criticism can help combat groupthink, make it easier to anticipate unintended consequences, and help teams avoid giving too much weight to leaders' opinions. Leaders also must push people to consider the impact of decisions on various stakeholders and deliberately break out of siloed perspectives.

These kinds of discussions can help ensure the thoughtful weighing of evidence. But all too often they get derailed even when they would be productive. Countless studies have shown that hierarchies can lead people to withhold dissenting views and that discussion participants tend to shy away from sharing potentially relevant data or asking probing questions when they don't experience *psychological safety*—the belief that candor is expected and won't be punished. Without psychological safety, the approach we've described is less likely to work.

Teams benefit when their members feel that offering up data, ideas, concerns, and alternative views will be valued by their peers and managers alike. Most important, in many discussions, participants should view asking probing questions as part of their job.

Much has been written about how to build psychological safety in a team. (See "Why Employees Are Afraid to Speak," by James R. Detert and Amy C. Edmondson, HBR, May 2007.)

But it's especially critical to establish it in a team that seeks to use evidence to make business decisions—so that the fear of raising unpopular findings doesn't cause members to miss critical data.

The chilling effect of low psychological safety was evident in the response to experimental research at Facebook that looked at whether showing more positive versus negative posts affected users' emotions. In 2014, in the aftermath of public backlash to the research—which arose partly because people didn't know that Facebook was running these types of experiments—CEO Mark Zuckerberg pulled the plug on ongoing external-facing research projects. That deterred employees from undertaking experiments that might explore Facebook's social impact proactively. More recently, Zuckerberg has changed course and expressed renewed interest in external research. However, had he created an atmosphere where Facebook executives felt able to thoughtfully discuss the negative effects of social media a decade ago, the company might have avoided some of its recent reputational challenges related to misinformation and its effects on user well-being.

From Data to Decisions

Decision-making in the face of uncertainty is necessarily iterative; it requires regular pauses for reflection on both information and process. Effective teams will learn from data, adjust plans accordingly, and deliberately work on improving their discussions.

Taking the time to discuss the nuances of analyses—including the sample size and composition, the outcomes being measured, the approach to separating causation from correlation, and the extent to which results might generalize from one setting to another—is vital to understanding how evidence can, or can't, inform a specific decision. When carefully considered, each empirical result presents a piece of a puzzle, helping businesses figure out whether and when different changes are likely to have an effect. Such discussions will also set the stage for organizations to be more rigorous about data collection.

Even in the best of worlds, evidence is rarely definitive, and how a business move will play out is uncertain. You can nonetheless aspire to make thoughtful choices based on information you have or might obtain. By employing a systematic approach to its collection, analysis, and interpretation, you can more effectively reap the benefits of the ever-increasing mountain of internal and external data and make better decisions.

Originally published in September–October 2024. Reprint R2405D

Making Better Decisions with Less Data

by Tanya Menon and Leigh Thompson

Maria, an executive in financial services, stared at another calendar invite in Outlook that would surely kill three hours of her day. Whenever a tough problem presented itself, her boss's knee-jerk response was, "Collect more data!" Maria appreciated her boss's analytical approach, but as the surveys, reports, and stats began to pile up, it was clear that the team was stuck in analysis paralysis. And despite the many meetings, task forces, brainstorming sessions, and workshops created to solve any given issue, the team tended to offer the same solutions—often ones that were recycled from prior problems.

As part of our research for our book, *Stop Spending, Start Managing,* we asked 83 executives how much they estimated that their companies wasted on relentless analytics on a daily basis. They reported a whopping $7,731 per day—$2,822,117 per year! Yet despite all of the data available, people often struggle to convert it into effective solutions to problems. Instead, they fall prey to what Jim March and his coauthors describe as "garbage can" decision-making: a process whereby actors, problems, and possible solutions swirl about in a metaphorical garbage can and people end up agreeing on whatever solution rises to the top. The problem isn't a *lack* of data inside the garbage can; the vast amount of data means managers struggle to prioritize what's important. In the end, they end up applying arbitrary data toward new problems, reaching a subpar solution.

To curb garbage-can decision-making, managers and their teams should think more carefully about the information they need to solve a problem and think more strategically about how to apply it to their decision-making and actions. We recommend the DIET approach. This method provides four steps of intentional thought to help convert data into knowledge and wisdom.

Step 1: Define

When teams and individuals think about a problem, they are likely to jump right into suggesting possible solutions. It's the basis of many brainstorming sessions. But while the prospect of problem-solving sounds positive, people tend to fixate on familiar approaches rather than stepping back to understand the contours of the problem.

Start with a problem-finding mindset, where you loosen the definitions around the problem and allow people to see it from different angles, thereby exposing hidden assumptions and revealing new questions before the hunt for data begins. With your team, think of critical questions about the problem to fully understand its complexity: How do you understand the problem? What are its causes? What assumptions does your team have? Alternatively, write about the problem (without proposing solutions) from

Idea in Brief

The Challenge

In an age of data abundance, many leaders delay decisions in pursuit of more information, believing that additional data always leads to better outcomes. But in fast-moving environments, waiting for perfect information can slow progress and stifle innovation.

The Insight

Great decision-makers know that getting more data isn't always the answer. To make better decisions with less information, focus on clarifying the decision's purpose, identifying key variables, and using heuristics or past experience to guide action. Embrace uncertainty as a natural part of decision-making, and build confidence through iteration and learning—not just analysis.

The Implications

Leaders who learn to decide with limited data can move faster, adapt more easily, and lead with greater clarity.

different perspectives—the customer, the supplier, and the competitor, for example—to see the situation in new ways.

Once you have a better view of the problem, you can move forward with a disciplined data search. Avoid decision-making delays by holding data requests accountable to if-then statements. Ask yourself a simple question: If I collect the data, then how would my decision change? If the data won't change your decision, you don't need to track down the additional information.

Step 2: Integrate

Once you've defined the problem and the data you need, you must use that information effectively. In the preceding example, Maria felt frustrated because, as the team members collected

more and more pieces of the jigsaw puzzle, they weren't investing the same amount of time to see how the pieces fit together.
Their subconscious beliefs or assumptions about problems
guided their behavior, causing them to follow the same tired
routine time and again: Collect data, hold meetings, create strategy moving forward. But this routine is garbage-can decision-
making. To keep the pieces from coming together in an arbitrary
fashion, you need to look at the data differently.

Integration lets you analyze how your problem and the data
fit together, and this process then lets you break down your hidden assumptions. With your team, create a KJ diagram (named
after author Kawakita Jiro) to sort facts into causal relationships.
Write the facts on notecards, and then sort them into piles based
on observable relationships—for example, an increase in clients
after a successful initiative, a drop in sales caused by a delayed
project, or any other data points that may indicate correlated
items or causal relationships. In doing this, you can create a
visual model of the patterns that emerge and make connections
in the data.

Step 3: Explore

At this point in the process, you may have developed some initial ideas or solutions from your KJ diagrams. Now's the time
to develop them. To facilitate collaborative exploration, one of
our favorite exercises (often used in art schools) is what we call
the passing game. Assign distinct ideas to each team member,
and give each individual five minutes to develop it by drawing or writing in silence. Then have them pass their work to a

teammate, who continues drafting the idea while they take over another teammate's creation.

Discuss the collaborative output. Teammates recognize how it feels to give up ownership of an idea and how it feels to both edit and be edited; they also recognize their implicit assumptions about collaboration. The new perspective forces them to confront directions that they didn't choose or never would have considered. Indeed, you can add multiple sequential passes (like a telephone game) to demonstrate the idea's unpredictable evolution as three or four teammates play with the initial ideas. After allowing people this space for exploration, discuss the directions that are most fruitful.

Step 4: Test

The last dimension requires team members to use their powers of critical thinking to consider feasibility and to correct for overreach. Design tests to see if your plan will work. Under which types of situations will the solution fail? Select a few critical tests and run them. While people often over-collect data that supports their priors, people under-collect disconfirming data. By running even a single test that fights confirmation biases, you can see what you need to see, even if you don't want to.

. . .

The solution to garbage-can decisions isn't cutting out data entirely. Thinking strategically about your data needs pushes you to do more with less—widening, deepening, integrating, extending, and testing the data you do have to convert it into knowledge and wisdom. In practicing the preceding mental exercises with your team, you can curb your appetite for data while getting better at digesting the data you already have.

Adapted from "How to Make Better Decisions with Less Data" on hbr.org, November 7, 2016 (reprint #H038UJ)

7

Who Has the D?

How Clear Decision Roles Enhance Organizational Performance

by Paul Rogers and Marcia W. Blenko

Decisions are the coin of the realm in business. Every success, every mishap, every opportunity seized or missed is the result of a decision that someone made or failed to make. At many companies, decisions routinely get stuck inside the organization like loose change. But it's more than loose change that's at stake, of course; it's the performance of the entire organization. Never mind what industry you're in, how big and well known your company may be, or how clever your strategy is. If you can't make the right decisions quickly and effectively, and execute those decisions consistently, your business will lose ground.

Indeed, making good decisions and making them happen quickly are the hallmarks of high-performing organizations. When we surveyed executives at 350 global companies about their organizational effectiveness, only 15% said that they have an organization that helps the business outperform competitors. What sets those top performers apart is the quality, speed, and execution of their decision making. The most effective organizations score well on the major strategic decisions—which markets to enter or exit, which businesses to buy or sell, where to allocate capital and talent. But they truly shine when it comes to the critical operating decisions requiring consistency and speed—how to drive product innovation, the best way to position brands, how to manage channel partners.

Even in companies respected for their decisiveness, however, there can be ambiguity over who is accountable for which decisions. As a result, the entire decision-making process can stall, usually at one of four bottlenecks: global versus local, center versus business unit, function versus function, and inside versus outside partners.

The first of these bottlenecks, *global versus local* decision making, can occur in nearly every major business process and function. Decisions about brand building and product development frequently get snared here, when companies wrestle over how much authority local businesses should have to tailor products for their markets. Marketing is another classic global versus local issue—should local markets have the power to determine pricing and advertising?

The second bottleneck, *center versus business unit* decision making, tends to afflict parent companies and their subsidiaries. Business units are on the front line, close to the customer; the center sees the big picture, sets broad goals, and keeps the organization focused on winning. Where should the decision-making power lie? Should a major capital investment, for example, depend on the approval of the business unit that will own it, or should headquarters make the final call?

Idea in Brief

Decisions are the coin of the realm in business. Every success, every mishap, every opportunity seized or missed stems from a decision someone made—or failed to make. Yet in many firms, decisions routinely stall inside the organization—hurting the entire company's performance.

The culprit? Ambiguity over who's accountable for which decisions. In one auto manufacturer that was missing milestones for rolling out new models, marketers *and* product developers each thought they were responsible for deciding new models' standard features and colors. Result? Conflict over who had final say, endless revisiting of decisions—and missed deadlines that led to lost sales.

How to clarify decision accountability? Assign clear roles for the decisions that most affect your firm's performance—such as which markets to enter, where to allocate capital, and how to drive product innovation. Think "RAPID": Who should recommend a course of action on a key decision? Who must agree to a recommendation before it can move forward? Who will perform the actions needed to implement the decision? Whose input is needed to determine the proposal's feasibility? Who decides—brings the decision to closure and commits the organization to implement it?

When you clarify decision roles, you make the *right* choices—swiftly and effectively.

Function versus function decision making is perhaps the most common bottleneck. Every manufacturer, for instance, faces a balancing act between product development and marketing during the design of a new product. Who should decide what? Cross-functional decisions too often result in ineffective compromise solutions, which frequently need to be revisited because the right people were not involved at the outset.

The fourth decision-making bottleneck, *inside versus outside partners*, has become familiar with the rise of outsourcing, joint ventures, strategic alliances, and franchising. In such arrangements, companies need to be absolutely clear about which decisions can be owned by the external partner (usually those about the execution of strategy) and which must continue to be made internally (decisions about the strategy itself). In the case of outsourcing, for instance, brand-name apparel and footwear marketers once assumed that overseas suppliers could be responsible for decisions about plant employees' wages and working conditions. Big mistake.

Clearing the Bottlenecks

The most important step in unclogging decision-making bottlenecks is assigning clear roles and responsibilities. Good decision makers recognize which decisions really matter to performance. They think through who should recommend a particular path, who needs to agree, who should have input, who has ultimate responsibility for making the decision, and who is accountable for follow-through. They make the process routine. The result: better coordination and quicker response times.

Companies have devised a number of methods to clarify decision roles and assign responsibilities. We have used an approach called RAPID, which has evolved over the years, to help hundreds of companies develop clear decision-making guidelines. It is, for sure, not a panacea (an indecisive decision maker, for example, can ruin any good system), but it's an important start. The letters in RAPID stand for the primary roles in any decision-making process, although these roles are not performed exactly in this order: recommend, agree, perform, input, and decide—the "D." (See the sidebar "A Decision-Making Primer.")

The people who *recommend* a course of action are responsible for making a proposal or offering alternatives. They need data and analysis to support their recommendations, as well as common sense about what's reasonable, practical, and effective.

The people who *agree* to a recommendation are those who need to sign off on it before it can move forward. If they veto a proposal, they must either work with the recommender to come up with an alternative or elevate the issue to the person with the D. For decision making to function smoothly, only a few people should have such veto power. They may be executives responsible for legal or regulatory compliance or the heads of units whose operations will be significantly affected by the decision.

People with *input* responsibilities are consulted about the recommendation. Their role is to provide the relevant facts that are the basis of any good decision: How practical is the proposal? Can manufacturing accommodate the design change? Where there's dissent or contrasting views, it's important to get these people to the table at the right time. The recommender has no obligation to act on the input he or she receives but is expected to take it into account—particularly since the people who provide input are generally among those who must implement a decision. Consensus is a worthy goal, but as a decision-making standard, it can be an obstacle to action or a recipe for lowest-common-denominator compromise. A more practical objective is to get everyone involved to buy in to the decision.

Eventually, one person will *decide*. The decision maker is the single point of accountability who must bring the decision to closure and commit the organization to act on it. To be strong and effective, the person with the D needs good business judgment, a grasp of the relevant trade-offs, a bias for action, and a keen awareness of the organization that will execute the decision.

The final role in the process involves the people who will *perform* the decision. They see to it that the decision is implemented promptly and effectively. It's a crucial role. Very often, a good decision executed quickly beats a brilliant decision implemented slowly or poorly.

RAPID can be used to help redesign the way an organization works or to target a single bottleneck. Some companies use the approach for the top 10 to 20 decisions, or just for the CEO and his or her direct reports. Other companies use it throughout the organization—to improve customer service by clarifying decision roles on the front line, for instance. When people see an effective process for making decisions, they spread the word. For example, after senior managers at a major U.S. retailer used RAPID to sort out a particularly thorny set of corporate decisions, they promptly built the process into their own functional organizations.

To see the process in action, let's look at the way four companies have worked through their decision-making bottlenecks.

Global Versus Local

Every major company today operates in global markets, buying raw materials in one place, shipping them somewhere else, and selling finished products all over the world. Most are trying simultaneously to build local presence and expertise, and to achieve economies of scale. Decision making in this environment is far from straightforward. Frequently, decisions cut across the boundaries between global and local managers, and sometimes across a regional layer in between: What investments will streamline our supply chain? How far should we go in standardizing products or tailoring them for local markets?

The trick in decision making is to avoid becoming either mindlessly global or hopelessly local. If decision-making authority tilts too far toward global executives, local customers' preferences

A Decision-Making Primer

Good decision making depends on assigning clear and specific roles. This sounds simple enough, but many companies struggle to make decisions because lots of people feel accountable—or no one does. RAPID and other tools used to analyze decision making give senior management teams a method for assigning roles and involving the relevant people. The key is to be clear who has input, who gets to decide, and who gets it done.

The five letters in RAPID correspond to the five critical decision-making roles: recommend, agree, perform, input, and decide. As you'll see, the roles are not carried out lockstep in this order—we took some liberties for the sake of creating a useful acronym.

Recommend

People in this role are responsible for making a proposal, gathering input, and providing the right data and analysis to make a sensible decision in a timely fashion. In the course of developing a proposal, recommenders consult with the people who provide input, not just hearing and incorporating their views but also building buy in along the way. Recommenders must have analytical skills, common sense, and organizational smarts.

Agree

Individuals in this role have veto power—yes or no—over the recommendation. Exercising the veto triggers a debate between themselves and the recommenders, which should lead to a modified proposal. If that takes too long, or if the two parties simply can't agree, they can escalate the issue to the person who has the D.

Input

These people are consulted on the decision. Because the people who provide input are typically involved in implementation,

(continued)

recommenders have a strong interest in taking their advice seriously. No input is binding, but this shouldn't undermine its importance. If the right people are not involved and motivated, the decision is far more likely to falter during execution.

Decide

The person with the D is the formal decision maker. He or she is ultimately accountable for the decision, for better or worse, and has the authority to resolve any impasse in the decision-making process and to commit the organization to action.

Perform

Once a decision is made, a person or group of people will be responsible for executing it. In some instances, the people responsible for implementing a decision are the same people who recommended it.

Writing down the roles and assigning accountability are essential steps, but good decision making also requires the right process. Too many rules can cause the process to collapse under its own weight. The most effective process is grounded in specifics but simple enough to adapt if necessary.

When the process gets slowed down, the problem can often be traced back to one of three trouble spots. First is a lack of clarity about who has the D. If more than one person think they have it for a particular decision, that decision will get caught up in a tug-of-war. The flip side can be equally damaging: No one is accountable for crucial decisions, and the business suffers. Second, a proliferation of people who have veto power can make life tough for recommenders. If a company has too many people in the "agree" role, it usually means that decisions are not pushed down far enough in the organization. Third, if there are a lot of people giving input, it's a signal that at least some of them aren't making a meaningful contribution.

can easily be overlooked, undermining the efficiency and agility of local operations. But with too much local authority, a company is likely to miss out on crucial economies of scale or opportunities with global clients.

To strike the right balance, a company must recognize its most important sources of value and make sure that decision roles line up with them. This was the challenge facing Martin Broughton, the former CEO and chairman of British American Tobacco, the second-largest tobacco company in the world. In 1993, when Broughton was appointed chief executive, BAT was losing ground to its nearest competitor. Broughton knew that the company needed to take better advantage of its global scale, but decision roles and responsibilities were at odds with this goal. Four geographic operating units ran themselves autonomously, rarely collaborating and sometimes even competing. Achieving consistency across global brands proved difficult, and cost synergies across the operating units were elusive. Industry insiders joked that "there are seven major tobacco companies in the world—and four of them are British American Tobacco." Broughton vowed to change the punch line.

The chief executive envisioned an organization that could take advantage of the opportunities a global business offers— global brands that could compete with established winners such as Altria Group's Marlboro; global purchasing of important raw materials, including tobacco; and more consistency in innovation and customer management. But Broughton didn't want the company to lose its nimbleness and competitive hunger in local markets by shifting too much decision-making power to global executives.

The first step was to clarify roles for the most important decisions. Procurement became a proving ground. Previously, each operating unit had identified its own suppliers and negotiated contracts for all materials. Under Broughton, a global procurement team was set up in headquarters and given authority to choose suppliers and negotiate pricing and quality for global materials, including bulk tobacco and certain types of packaging. Regional procurement teams were now given input into global materials strategies but ultimately had to implement the team's decision. As soon as the global team signed contracts with suppliers, responsibility shifted to the regional teams, who worked out the details of delivery and service with the suppliers in their regions. For materials that did not offer global economies of scale (mentholated filters for the North American market, for example), the regional teams retained their decision-making authority.

As the effort to revamp decision making in procurement gained momentum, the company set out to clarify roles in all its major decisions. The process wasn't easy. A company the size of British American Tobacco has a huge number of moving parts, and developing a practical system for making decisions requires sweating lots of details. What's more, decision-making authority is power, and people are often reluctant to give it up.

It's crucial for the people who will live with the new system to help design it. At BAT, Broughton created working groups led by people earmarked, implicitly or explicitly, for leadership roles in the future. For example, Paul Adams, who ultimately succeeded Broughton as chief executive, was asked to lead the group charged with redesigning decision making for brand and customer management. At the time, Adams was a regional head within one of the operating units. With other senior executives, including some of his own direct reports, Broughton specified that their role was to provide input, not to veto recommendations. Broughton didn't make the common mistake of seeking consensus, which is often an obstacle to action. Instead, he made it clear that the objective was not deciding whether to change the decision-making process but achieving buy-in about how to do so as effectively as possible.

The new decision roles provided the foundation the company needed to operate successfully on a global basis while retaining flexibility at the local level. The focus and efficiency of its decision making were reflected in the company's results: After the decision-making overhaul, British American Tobacco experienced nearly 10 years of growth well above the levels of its competitors in sales, profits, and market value. The company has gone on to have one of the best-performing stocks on the UK market and has reemerged as a major global player in the tobacco industry.

Center Versus Business Unit

The first rule for making good decisions is to involve the right people at the right level of the organization. For BAT, capturing economies of scale required its global team to appropriate some decision-making powers from regional divisions. For many companies, a similar balancing act takes place between executives at the center and managers in the business units. If too many decisions flow to the center, decision making can grind to a halt. The problem is different but no less critical if the decisions that are elevated to senior executives are the wrong ones.

Companies often grow into this type of problem. In small and midsize organizations, a single management team—sometimes a single leader—effectively handles every major decision. As a company grows and its operations become more complex, however, senior executives can no longer master the details required to make decisions in every business.

A change in management style, often triggered by the arrival of a new CEO, can create similar tensions. At a large British retailer, for example, the senior team was accustomed to the founder making all critical decisions. When his successor began seeking consensus on important issues, the team was suddenly unsure of its role, and many decisions stalled. It's a common scenario, yet most management teams and boards of directors don't specify how decision-making authority should change as the company does.

A growth opportunity highlighted that issue for Wyeth (then known as American Home Products) in late 2000. Through organic growth, acquisitions, and partnerships, Wyeth's pharmaceutical division had developed three sizable businesses: biotech, vaccines, and traditional pharmaceutical products. Even though each business had its own market dynamics, operating requirements, and research focus, most important decisions were pushed up to one group of senior executives. "We were using generalists across all issues," said Joseph M. Mahady, president of North American and global businesses for Wyeth Pharmaceuticals. "It was a signal that we weren't getting our best decision making."

The problem crystallized for Wyeth when managers in the biotech business saw a vital—but perishable—opportunity to establish a leading position with Enbrel, a promising rheumatoid arthritis drug. Competitors were working on the same class of drug, so Wyeth needed to move quickly. This meant expanding production capacity by building a new plant, which would be located at the Grange Castle Business Park in Dublin, Ireland.

The decision, by any standard, was a complex one. Once approved by regulators, the facility would be the biggest biotech plant in the world—and the largest capital investment

Wyeth had ever undertaken. Yet peak demand for the drug was not easy to determine. What's more, Wyeth planned to market Enbrel in partnership with Immunex (now a part of Amgen). In its deliberations about the plant, therefore, Wyeth needed to factor in the requirements of building up its technical expertise, technology transfer issues, and an uncertain competitive environment.

Input on the decision filtered up slowly through a gauze of overlapping committees, leaving senior executives hungry for a more detailed grasp of the issues. Given the narrow window of opportunity, Wyeth acted quickly, moving from a first look at the Grange Castle project to implementation in six months. But in the midst of this process, Wyeth Pharmaceuticals' executives saw the larger issue: The company needed a system that would push more decisions down to the business units, where operational knowledge was greatest, and elevate the decisions that required the senior team's input, such as marketing strategy and manufacturing capacity.

In short order, Wyeth gave authority for many decisions to business unit managers, leaving senior executives with veto power over some of the more sensitive issues related to Grange Castle. But after that investment decision was made, the D for many subsequent decisions about the Enbrel business lay with Cavan Redmond, the executive vice president and general manager of Wyeth's biotech division, and his new management team. Redmond gathered input from managers in biotech manufacturing, marketing, forecasting, finance, and R&D, and quickly set up the complex schedules needed to collaborate with Immunex. Responsibility for execution rested firmly with the business unit, as always. But now Redmond, supported by his team, also had authority to make important decisions.

Grange Castle is paying off so far. Enbrel is among the leading brands for rheumatoid arthritis, with sales of $1.7 billion through the first half of 2005. And Wyeth's metabolism for making decisions has increased. Recently, when the U.S. Food and Drug Administration granted priority review status to another new drug, Tygacil, because of the antibiotic's efficacy against drug-resistant infections, Wyeth displayed its new reflexes. To keep Tygacil on a fast track, the company had to orchestrate a host of critical steps—refining the process technology, lining up supplies, ensuring quality control, allocating manufacturing capacity. The vital decisions were made one or two levels down in the biotech organization, where the expertise resided. "Instead of debating whether you can move your product into my shop, we had the decision systems in place to run it up and down the business units and move ahead rapidly with Tygacil," said Mahady. The drug was approved by the FDA in June 2005 and moved into volume production a mere three days later.

Function Versus Function

Decisions that cut across functions are some of the most important a company faces. Indeed, cross-functional collaboration has become an axiom of business, essential for arriving at the best answers for the company and its customers. But fluid decision making across functional teams remains a constant challenge, even for companies known for doing it well, like Toyota and Dell. For instance, a team that thinks it's more efficient to make a decision without consulting other functions may wind up missing out on relevant input or being overruled by another team that believes—rightly or wrongly—it should have been included

A Recipe for a Decision-Making Bottleneck

At one automaker we studied, marketers and product developers were confused about who was responsible for making decisions about new models.

When we asked, "Who has the right to decide which features will be standard?"

64% of product developers said, "We do."

83% of marketers said, "We do."

When we asked, "Who has the right to decide which colors will be offered?"

77% of product developers said, "We do."

61% of marketers said, "We do."

Not surprisingly, the new models were delayed.

in the process. Many of the most important cross-functional decisions are, by their very nature, the most difficult to orchestrate, and that can string out the process and lead to sparring between fiefdoms and costly indecision.

The theme here is a lack of clarity about who has the D. For example, at a global auto manufacturer that was missing its milestones for rolling out new models—and was paying the price in falling sales—it turned out that marketers and product developers were confused about which function was responsible for making decisions about standard features and color ranges for new models. When we asked the marketing team who had the D about which features should be standard, 83% said the marketers did. When we posed the same question to product developers, 64% said the responsibility rested with them. (See "A Recipe for a Decision-Making Bottleneck.")

The practical difficulty of connecting functions through smooth decision making crops up frequently at retailers. John Lewis, the leading department store chain in the United Kingdom, might reasonably expect to overcome this sort of challenge more readily than other retailers. Spedan Lewis, who built the business in the early 20th century, was a pioneer in employee ownership. A strong connection between managers and employees permeated every aspect of the store's operations and remained vital to the company as it grew into the largest employee-owned business in the United Kingdom, with 59,600 employees and more than £5 billion in revenues in 2004.

Even at John Lewis, however, with its heritage of cooperation and teamwork, cross-functional decision making can be hard to sustain. Take salt and pepper mills, for instance. John Lewis, which prides itself on having great selection, stocked nearly 50 SKUs of salt and pepper mills, while most competitors stocked around 20. The company's buyers saw an opportunity to increase sales and reduce complexity by offering a smaller number of popular and well-chosen products in each price point and style.

When John Lewis launched the new range, sales fell. This made no sense to the buyers until they visited the stores and saw how the merchandise was displayed. The buyers had made their decision without fully involving the sales staff, who therefore did not understand the strategy behind the new selection. As a result, the sellers had cut shelf space in half to match the reduction in range, rather than devoting the same amount of shelf space to stocking more of each product.

To fix the communication problem, John Lewis needed to clarify decision roles. The buyers were given the D on how much space to allocate to each product category. If the space allocation didn't make sense to the sales staff, however, they had the authority to raise their concerns and force a new round of negotiations. They also had responsibility for implementing product layouts in the stores. When the communication was sorted out and shelf space was restored, sales of the salt and pepper mills climbed well above original levels.

Crafting a decision-making process that connected the buying and selling functions for salt and pepper mills was relatively easy; rolling it out across the entire business was more challenging. Salt and pepper mills are just one of several hundred product categories for John Lewis. This element of scale is one reason why cross-functional bottlenecks are not easy to unclog. Different functions have different incentives and goals, which are often in conflict. When it comes down to a struggle between two functions, there may be good reasons to locate the D in either place—buying or selling, marketing or product development.

Here, as elsewhere, someone needs to think objectively about where value is created and assign decision roles accordingly. Eliminating cross-functional bottlenecks actually has less to do with shifting decision-making responsibilities between departments and more to do with ensuring that the people with relevant information are allowed to share it. The decision maker is important, of course, but more important is designing a system that aligns decision making and makes it routine.

Inside Versus Outside Partners

Decision making within an organization is hard enough. Trying to make decisions between separate organizations on different continents adds layers of complexity that can scuttle the best strategy. Companies that outsource capabilities in pursuit of cost and quality advantages face this very challenge. Which

The Decision-Driven Organization

The defining characteristic of high-performing organizations is their ability to make good decisions and to make them happen quickly. The companies that succeed tend to follow a few clear principles.

Some decisions matter more than others

The decisions that are crucial to building value in the business are the ones that matter most. Some of them will be the big strategic decisions, but just as important are the critical operating decisions that drive the business day-to-day and are vital to effective execution.

Action is the goal

Good decision making doesn't end with a decision; it ends with implementation. The objective shouldn't be consensus, which often becomes an obstacle to action, but buy-in.

Ambiguity is the enemy

Clear accountability is essential: Who contributes input, who makes the decision, and who carries it out? Without clarity, gridlock and delay are the most likely outcomes. Clarity doesn't necessarily mean concentrating authority in a few people; it means defining who has responsibility to make decisions, who has input, and who is charged with putting them into action.

decisions should be made internally? Which can be delegated to outsourcing partners?

These questions are also relevant for strategic partners—a global bank working with an IT contractor on a systems development project, for example, or a media company that acquires content from a studio—and for companies conducting part of

Speed and adaptability are crucial

A company that makes good decisions quickly has a higher metabolism, which allows it to act on opportunities and overcome obstacles. The best decision makers create an environment where people can come together quickly and efficiently to make the most important decisions.

Decision roles trump the organizational chart

No decision-making structure will be perfect for every decision. The key is to involve the right people at the right level in the right part of the organization at the right time.

A well-aligned organization reinforces roles

Clear decision roles are critical, but they are not enough. If an organization does not reinforce the right approach to decision making through its measures and incentives, information flows, and culture, the behavior won't become routine.

Practicing beats preaching

Involve the people who will live with the new decision roles in designing them. The very process of thinking about new decision behaviors motivates people to adopt them.

their business through franchisees. There is no right answer to who should have the power to decide what. But the wrong approach is to assume that contractual arrangements can provide the answer.

An outdoor-equipment company based in the United States discovered this recently when it decided to scale up production of gas patio heaters for the lower end of the market. The company had some success manufacturing high-end products in China. But with the advent of superdiscounters like Walmart, Target,

A Decision Diagnostic

Consider the last three meaningful decisions you've been involved in and ask yourself the following questions.

1. Were the decisions right?

2. Were they made with appropriate speed?

3. Were they executed well?

4. Were the right people involved, in the right way?

5. Was it clear for each decision . . .

   - who would recommend a solution?

   - who would provide input?

   - who had the final say?

   - who would be responsible for following through?

6. Were the decision roles, process, and time frame respected?

7. Were the decisions based on appropriate facts?

8. To the extent that there were divergent facts or opinions, was it clear who had the D?

9. Were the decision makers at the appropriate level in the company?

10. Did the organization's measures and incentives encourage the people involved to make the right decisions?

and Home Depot, the company realized it needed to move more of its production overseas to feed these retailers with lower-cost offerings. The timetable left little margin for error: The company started tooling up factories in April and June of 2004, hoping to be ready for the Christmas season.

Right away, there were problems. Although the Chinese manufacturing partners understood costs, they had little idea what American consumers wanted. When expensive designs arrived from the head office in the United States, Chinese plant managers made compromises to meet contracted cost targets. They used a lower-grade material, which discolored. They placed the power switch in a spot that was inconvenient for the user but easier to build. Instead of making certain parts from a single casting, they welded materials together, which looked terrible.

To fix these problems, the U.S. executives had to draw clear lines around which decisions should be made on which side of the ocean. The company broke down the design and manufacturing process into five steps and analyzed how decisions were made at each step. The company was also much more explicit about what the manufacturing specs would include and what the manufacturer was expected to do with them. The objective was not simply to clarify decision roles but to make sure those roles corresponded directly to the sources of value in the business. If a decision would affect the look and feel of the finished product, headquarters would have to sign off on it. But if a decision would not affect the customer's experience, it could be made in China. If, for example, Chinese engineers found a less expensive material that didn't compromise the product's look, feel, and functionality, they could make that change on their own.

To help with the transition to this system, the company put a team of engineers on-site in China to ensure a smooth handoff of the specs and to make decisions on issues that would become complex and time-consuming if elevated to the home office. Marketing executives in the home office insisted that it should take a customer 10 minutes and no more than six steps to assemble the product at home. The company's engineers in China, along with the Chinese manufacturing team, had input into this assembly requirement and were responsible for execution. But the D resided with headquarters, and the requirement became a major design factor. Decisions about logistics, however, became the province of the engineering team in China: It would figure out how to package the heaters so that one-third more boxes would fit into a container, which reduced shipping costs substantially.

. . .

If managers suddenly realize that they're spending less time sitting through meetings wondering why they are there, that's an early signal that companies have become better at making decisions. When meetings start with a common understanding about who is responsible for providing valuable input and who has the D, an organization's decision-making metabolism will get a boost.

No single lever turns a decision-challenged organization into a decision-driven one, of course, and no blueprint can provide for all the contingencies and business shifts a company is bound to encounter. The most successful companies use simple tools that help them recognize potential bottlenecks and think through decision roles and responsibilities with each change in the business environment. That's difficult to do—and even more difficult for competitors to copy. But by taking some very practical steps, any company can become more effective, beginning with its next decision.

Originally published in January 2006. Reprint R0601D

8

Beyond the Echo Chamber

by Alex "Sandy" Pentland

The rap on decision making is that it's hard. Sure, there may be a few superbright people with an almost magical ability to consistently do it well, but the rest of us just get by. That is not what my colleagues and I have discovered in our research, however. We have seen that almost anyone can learn to be a good decision maker—and that the key to it is carefully and continually engaging in something we call *social exploration*.

Social explorers spend enormous amounts of time searching for new people and ideas—but not necessarily the *best* people or ideas. Instead, they seek to form connections with many different kinds of people and to gain exposure to a broad variety of thinking.

Explorers winnow down the ideas they've gathered by bouncing them off other people to see which ones resonate. Generally, those ideas are microstrategies—examples of actions that might be taken, circumstances conducive to the action, and possible outcomes. Then, by assembling a great set of microstrategies, social explorers make good decisions.

But how exactly does the exploration process generate ideas that lead to the right decisions? And are certain techniques critical to successful exploration? In this article, we'll attempt to answer those two questions.

Patterns of Social Learning

Studies of primitive peoples reinforce the idea that social interactions are central to how humans gather information and make decisions. Ethnologists have found that almost all decisions affecting groups as a whole are made in social situations. (The major exception is during battles or other emergencies, when extremely rapid decision making is required.) This tendency evolved in humans because pooling ideas from many different people gave you an advantage: You got a "wisdom of the crowd" take on things that was better than individual judgment.

When field biologists observe animal populations, they see that social learning—which takes place primarily through the imitation of successful individuals—can improve success in foraging decisions, mate choice, and habitat selection. In both animals and humans, however, this effect occurs only as long as the individuals in the group have diverse strategies. Indeed, one key to good decision making is learning from the successes and failures of others—frequently and in a range of situations.

To understand how patterns of social learning work in a modern business environment, MIT postdoctoral associate Yaniv Altshuler and PhD student Wei Pan and I did a research project involving eToro, an online trading platform. eToro allows individual day

Idea in Brief

The Theory

The best decisions result from constant social exploration—the process of gathering, winnowing, and testing out ideas from other people. It allows decision makers to tap into the "wisdom of the crowd."

The Research

The author and his colleagues studied decision making on eToro, a social investment platform where traders can follow and copy one another's moves. They found that investors who paid attention to the trading strategies of a wide group of people (without following the herd) achieved the highest returns.

The Bottom Line

Decision makers need to tap diverse social networks. If your circle is too tight and the members of it are too similar, you risk being trapped in an echo chamber where the same ideas keep circulating, limiting the payoff of social learning.

traders to observe and copy one another's moves, portfolios, and past performance. Information on the site is extremely transparent, so it's easy to see and precisely measure how interactions affect decisions and results. On eToro, investors can do two main types of trades. A "single trade" is a normal stock purchase a user makes on his own. A "social trade" is when a user places a trade that exactly copies another user's single trade. Users can also "follow" all of another user's trades automatically and review all real-time trades and choose which ones to copy.

All users have to open up their trading decisions, share their strategies and ideas, and let other people follow them. Most users select several other traders to follow. Each time someone decides to copy another trader, that trader gets paid a small amount. Traders with a lot of imitators can make quite a bit of money.

During 2011, we collected data about euro/dollar trading from 1.6 million eToro users. In total we were able to examine almost 10 million financial transactions. The fascinating thing was that we could actually see social learning happen, track the effect it had on people's actions, and measure whether or not each action was profitable. There are few (if any) other data sets where you can see social exploration so clearly and determine which patterns of it work best.

If you look at a chart of investor behavior on eToro (see "Finding the decision-making sweet spot"), you can see that people fall along a continuum. One group of investors works in almost total isolation: Its members follow few other traders and come up with most investment ideas on their own. At the other end of this spectrum lies a group of hyperconnected traders who follow (and are followed by) many others, and social learning guides a lot of their strategies. Many of the investors using eToro fall somewhere in the middle—they engage in a moderate level of social learning but behave with a degree of independence that makes it clear that they're not just following the herd.

What pattern of exploration and social learning produced the best outcome? We discovered the answer when we plotted the return on investment each trader got against the diversity of ideas he or she harvested through social learning. An analysis of the results reveals that the effect of social learning is enormous. The traders who had the right balance and diversity of ideas in their network—meaning that their social learning was neither too sparse nor too dense—had a return on investment that was 30% higher than the returns of both the isolated traders and those in the herd. In this digital trading environment, the sweet spot resides between the two extremes. This intermediate zone is where social learning—that is, copying successful

Finding the decision-making sweet spot

Each dot on this map represents a trade made by one of 1.6 million investors on eToro—10 million trades in all. The same investors are represented on both the x axis, as traders, and the y axis, as people whose decisions were copied by other investors. The high density shows a cluster of people copying one another so much that the same ideas kept recirculating: Investor A followed B, who followed C, who followed A. Low density shows investors who made their own investment decisions and didn't copy many others. The investors in the middle drew ideas from a wide variety of other traders but didn't follow the herd.

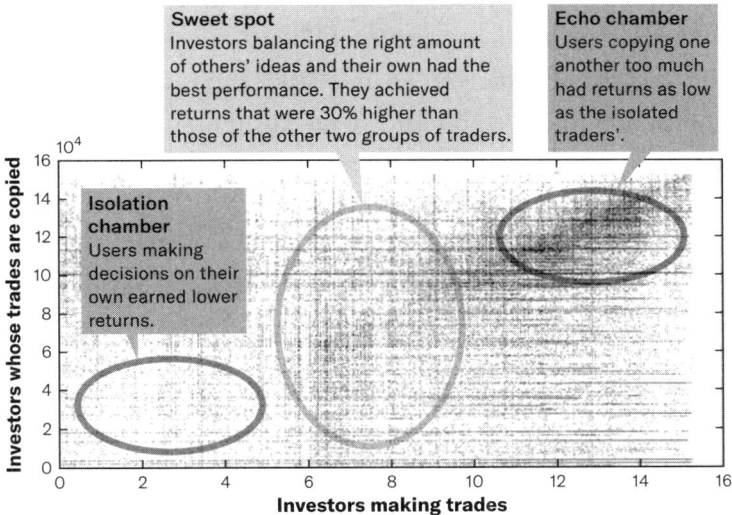

Sweet spot
Investors balancing the right amount of others' ideas and their own had the best performance. They achieved returns that were 30% higher than those of the other two groups of traders.

Echo chamber
Users copying one another too much had returns as low as the isolated traders'.

Isolation chamber
Users making decisions on their own earned lower returns.

y axis: **Investors whose trades are copied** (10^4), 0 to 16
x axis: **Investors making trades**, 0 to 16

people—yields real rewards. And though this study looked only at financial decision making, we believe the principle holds true for all kinds of decisions.

Idea Flow and Decision Making

The eToro study makes it very clear that the rate of idea flow is a critical measure of how well a social network functions in collecting and refining decision strategies. In my April 2012 HBR article, "The New Science of Building Great Teams," I showed that idea flow has two essential components—engagement *within* a group and exploration *outside* the group—and that it can predict both productivity and creative output.

But what can a single individual do to increase her rate of idea flow? A 1985 study that Robert Kelley of Carnegie Mellon University did at Bell Laboratories offers some insights. AT&T's famous research lab wanted to understand what separated a star performer from an average performer. Was it something innate, or could star performance be learned? Bell Labs already hired the best and the brightest, but only a few lived up to their apparent potential for brilliance. Most hires developed into solid performers but did not contribute substantially to AT&T's competitive advantage in the marketplace.

Kelley found that the best researchers engaged in "preparatory exploration"—that is, they proactively developed relationships and connections with other experts and later tapped them for help with completing critical tasks. Moreover, the social networks of the star performers were more diverse than the networks of the middling performers. Middling performers saw the world only from the viewpoint of their jobs and limited their social learning to people in similar roles—say, engineers. Stars, on the other hand, reached out to people from a broader set of work roles, so they understood the perspectives of customers, competitors, and managers. Because the stars could see the situation from a variety of viewpoints, they could develop better solutions to problems.

Organizations have ways of increasing idea flow, too. In studies of dozens of organizations, I have found that the number of opportunities for social learning (which usually involve informal face-to-face interactions among employees) is often the largest single factor in company productivity. In our research we assess the extent of such opportunities by measuring a group's engagement, or how much its members communicate with one another and whether all or just a few members are involved in the exchanges. The findings show that simple tricks to increase group engagement often have enormous payoffs. In one case a change in the coffee break timing allowed employees to talk more easily with one another, which resulted in productivity improvements that saved the company $15 million a year. Another company made its lunch tables longer, thus encouraging people who didn't know one another to interact more. That move alone increased productivity by an estimated 5%.

Idea flow is also affected by the way social learning interacts with individual learning. Decisions are a blend of personal and social information, and when personal information is weak, people tend to rely more on social information. When investors are uncertain about the market's direction, for instance, the effects of social learning become larger. Investors spend more time looking at what others are doing. And when people see others adopt trading strategies similar to their own, they often become more confident and are then likely to increase the amount they invest in those particular strategies.

This effect has a downside, however: It can lead to overconfidence and groupthink. Social learning improves decision making only when individuals each have different information. When the information from outside sources (such as magazines, TV, and radio) became too similar, we observed, social trading became reliably *unprofitable*. In such circumstances, not only does groupthink not pay, but betting against groupthink becomes a great trading strategy.

Similarly, when engagement is high and intensely concentrated within a group, the same ideas often circle around to you again and again. But because ideas usually change slightly as they go from person to person, you may not recognize them as mere repetitions of ideas. You may think that everyone has independently arrived at a similar strategy, which might make you more sure of those ideas than you should be. This "echo chamber" effect often leads to financial bubbles.

If you're aware of the echo chamber, though, you can avoid falling victim to it. You can observe how much influence people have on one another and watch for dependencies between people. Does team member A always vote the same way that team member B does? People who regularly have similar opinions probably have similar sources of information; the opinions of such "birds of a feather" can't really be considered independent. Tight social groups often experience echo chambers, since their members tend to share information, and there may be social pressure to hold the same opinions. By paying attention to idea flow within your network, you can discount repeated ideas and integrate opinions that are more likely to be truly independent.

Fine-Tuning a Network

A social network's structure, the degree of influence people have on one another, and individuals' susceptibility to new ideas all affect idea flow and thus the performance of the people in the network. By adjusting any of these variables, you can fine-tune social networks to produce better decisions and better results.

What can be done when, for example, the flow of ideas becomes either too sparse and slow, or too dense and fast? Among the members of eToro, we have found that we can alter the flow of ideas by providing small incentives or nudges to individuals, to encourage isolated traders to engage more with others, or traders who are too interconnected to engage less with the same group and explore outside their current contacts.

In one experiment with the eToro investors, Yaniv Altshuler and I used this approach to tune the social network so that it remained in the healthy "wisdom of the crowd" sweet spot—the range where traders had diverse opportunities for social learning but avoided the echo chamber. As a result, we were able to increase the profitability of all social traders by more than six percentage points—essentially doubling it. In fact, by managing idea flows, we were able to turn average traders—often the losers in our current financial system—into winners.

This tuning concept is applicable to all kinds of networks. Getting the right idea flow is critical in journalism (so reporters talk to enough sources to get all sides of a story), financial controls (to ensure that all sources of fraud have been considered), and ad campaigns (so companies sample a sufficiently diverse set of customer opinions). That's why Yaniv and I have created a spin-off company, called Athena Wisdom, that is now helping financial and decision-making networks around the world.

Our eToro research shows how social learning works in a very specific context: stock trading. But social learning also plays a key role in a wide variety of other managerial decisions. We are now examining its effects in organizational contexts like product planning, risk auditing, and information services, though that work is still in its infancy.

. . .

Decisions don't happen in a vacuum; the best ones rarely come from deep pondering in isolation. They happen when people learn from and draw on the experiences of others. In this process, success depends greatly on the quality of social exploration—and on whether your information and sources of ideas are diverse and independent.

Originally published in November 2013. Reprint R1311E

Five Questions to Help Your Team Make Better Decisions

by Steven Morris

Whether you're considering a career move or choosing a business strategy, the decisions you make today that will have short- and long-term effects on you, your team, and your organization require serious deliberation. They can't be made too quickly, nor can they be avoided. But in our fast-paced, complex business environment, it's often hard to carve out the time for thoughtful, thorough analysis that yields conclusive answers about the right path forward. We might recognize that better questions lead to better decisions, but we aren't sure exactly what to ask.

In my work, I help leaders tackle this problem by guiding them through a simple five-question framework designed to channel their focus and improve their processes. By using a few or all of these questions, you'll gain clarity, reduce risks, and set the foundation for better decisions and outcomes.

What Would Happen If We Did Nothing?

When opportunity knocks or industry dynamics are shifting, failure to act can be costly. But in some cases—for example, when you have incomplete information—it might be wiser to stay the course for now.

This question will prompt you to evaluate the mid- to long-term costs and benefits of inaction. Ask yourself or your team to imagine a future in which you haven't made any changes. Are you still successful? How have key stakeholders, like your family members (for career decisions) or your customers, employees, or investors (for business decisions), been affected? Is the pressure to do something based on complete data or a real need, or is it driven by short-term thinking and emotions?

What Could Make Us Regret This Decision?

As author Daniel Pink explains in his book *The Power of Regret,* most regrets fall into one of four categories: foundation (poor choices in education, health, or finances), boldness (missed opportunities or failure to take risks), moral (compromising our values or ethics), or connection (the risk of strained or lost relationships).

This question forces us to consider the potential adverse outcomes of a decision. Drill down with follow-ups like these: Is this a sound long-term choice for your physical, mental, and financial health? How likely are you to regret not being bold? Would a moral compromise lead to long-term dissatisfaction? Are you endangering a valued relationship? If this decision goes wrong, what would you regret the most? You can also reflect on past

Idea in Brief

The Problem

Teams often struggle to make high-quality decisions, especially under pressure or when navigating complex, ambiguous situations.

The Solution

Leaders can improve their teams' decision-making by asking five targeted questions that surface assumptions and encourage critical thinking: What would happen if we did nothing? What could make us regret this decision? What alternatives did we overlook? How will we know if this was the right decision? Is this decision reversible?

The Impact

By embedding these questions into their team's routines, leaders can avoid groupthink, clarify objectives, and foster a culture of thoughtful, transparent decision-making.

decisions that have led to regret, identify patterns, and learn from them.

What Alternatives Did We Overlook?

As self-aware as we try to be, our brains are wired for *confirmation bias*—favoring information that supports our beliefs—which can cause us to overlook other viable options. When teams are making decisions, it's likewise easy to drift into groupthink or settle on a course of action without fully exploring alternatives. Other blind spots include *anchoring bias*, when the first piece of information we get drives our decision; *sunk-cost fallacy*, when we stick with a choice because we've already invested resources in it; and *overconfidence bias*, when we assume we've got the right answer and so we stick with it.

This question is designed to disrupt these biases and keep you and your team curious. Consider additional courses of action, and ask whether they might yield better results. Revisit previously rejected paths, and ask whether your reasoning is still valid. Ask yourself and your colleagues whether all perspectives have been heard and all blind spots checked.

How Will We Know If This Was the Right Decision?

It's impossible to make a good decision if you or your team members aren't clear about what success looks like. You need a vision of the ideal outcome and clear metrics for desired performance, whether you obtain them through objectives and key results (OKRs); a balanced scorecard that tracks financial results, customer response, process efficiency, and growth; key performance indicators (KPIs); or specific, measurable, achievable, relevant, and time-bound (SMART) goals. Envision the results you expect from this decision. Find a progress-measurement system that looks at both the short and the long term. Set specific milestones. Make a plan for reviewing how quickly and successfully you're moving toward your goals.

Is This Decision Reversible?

By considering the reversibility or changeability of a decision, you can reduce the pressure to make the "perfect" choice. Especially in rapidly changing environments and complex projects, it might be possible to iterate, test, and course-correct, making multiple decisions toward a final solution.

Ask yourself or your team several key questions: What are the costs—both financial and reputational—of reversing the decision should you need to? How easy or difficult would it be to pivot? Can you break the move into smaller steps that would allow you to experiment and gather feedback? What signals, data, or metrics would tell you it's time to reconsider? What does your gut tell you about this decision?

Applying the Questions

A financial services company I work with was deciding whether to expand into a fintech solution model or continue with its service model. First, I worked with the leadership team to explore the consequences of inaction: Losing more tech-savvy customers and failing to keep pace with competitors were the two primary concerns. We also considered potential regrets, including missed market opportunities and the costs of investing in the wrong technology solution. Then we examined various alternatives, such as building hybrid technology and service tools and staying the course of going all-in on their current service model. Next, we outlined what success would look like using OKRs, which included revenue growth potential, cost-to-income ratios, and customer lifetime value of both the services model and the forecasted fintech solutions. We also looked at KPIs, including the percentage of customer retention, new customer acquisition costs and returns, and a customer success matrix. Finally, we considered how to take an agile approach to the technology development and rollout, breaking the potential project into a series of smaller go or no-go decisions.

Two years later, the financial services firm launched a beta version of its fintech platform, and new customer growth is climbing and current customer retention is positive.

Another case study comes from an executive I advise. She was offered a significant promotion by her *Fortune* 100 company just as she was contemplating leaving corporate life to pursue a career in writing and consulting. Through a series of coaching sessions, we applied the five-question framework. She focused mainly on the regret question and its follow-ups, which helped her assess how she would feel if she continued working at her employer rather than try something new. Would she look back in five or 10 years and wish she had taken the chance? Would she always wonder what could have been? Or would the stability and prestige of the new role ultimately bring her enough fulfillment?

We also did some scenario planning around how reversible the decision to leave could be. For example, if her entrepreneurial path didn't work out as expected, how easy or difficult would it be to reenter the corporate world? What professional relationships could she maintain as a safety net and a new career accelerant? Could she negotiate a consulting arrangement with her former employer to keep a financial cushion while she built her business? This work gave her the clarity and confidence to eschew the promotion and leave her job. She is now one year into her entrepreneurial and writing journey, with a speaking tour and book agent lined up, initial income targets exceeded, and, most importantly, a more satisfying lifestyle.

. . .

The preceding five questions can't guarantee you a good decision, but they can sharpen your decision-making process, whether in personal matters or business strategy. As you use them on your own and with your team over time, these questions will also help you foster the habits you need for long-term growth and success.

Adapted from content on hbr.org, February 7, 2025. Reprint H08M6L

9

Conquering a Culture of Indecision

by Ram Charan

Does this sound familiar? You're sitting in the quarterly business review as a colleague plows through a two-inch-thick proposal for a big investment in a new product. When he finishes, the room falls quiet. People look left, right, or down, waiting for someone else to open the discussion. No one wants to comment—at least not until the boss shows which way he's leaning.

Finally, the CEO breaks the loud silence. He asks a few mildly skeptical questions to show he's done his due diligence. But it's clear that he has made up his mind to back the project. Before long, the other meeting attendees are chiming in dutifully, careful to keep their comments positive. Judging from the remarks, it appears that everyone in the room supports the project.

But appearances can be deceiving. The head of a related division worries that the new product will take resources away from his operation. The vice president of manufacturing thinks that the first-year sales forecasts are wildly optimistic and will leave him with a warehouse full of unsold goods. Others in the room are lukewarm because they don't see how they stand to gain from the project. But they keep their reservations to themselves, and the meeting breaks up inconclusively. Over the next few months, the project is slowly strangled to death in a series of strategy, budget, and operational reviews. It's not clear who's responsible for the killing, but it's plain that the true sentiment in the room was the opposite of the apparent consensus.

In my career as an adviser to large organizations and their leaders, I have witnessed many occasions even at the highest levels when silent lies and a lack of closure lead to false decisions. They are "false" because they eventually get undone by unspoken factors and inaction. And after a quarter century of firsthand observations, I have concluded that these instances of indecision share a family resemblance—a misfire in the personal interactions that are supposed to produce results. The people charged with reaching a decision and acting on it fail to connect and engage with one another. Intimidated by the group dynamics of hierarchy and constrained by formality and lack of trust, they speak their lines woodenly and without conviction. Lacking emotional commitment, the people who must carry out the plan don't act decisively.

These faulty interactions rarely occur in isolation. Far more often, they're typical of the way large and small decisions are made—or not made—throughout a company. The inability to take decisive action is rooted in the corporate culture and seems to employees to be impervious to change.

The key word here is *seems*, because, in fact, leaders create a culture of indecisiveness, and leaders can break it. The primary instrument at their disposal is the human interactions—the

Idea in Brief

The Problem

Many organizations suffer from a culture of indecision, where teams delay or avoid making tough calls. It often stems from a fear of conflict, a desire for consensus, or unclear accountability—leading to stalled progress and missed opportunities.

The Solution

To break this cycle, leaders must foster a culture of decisive dialogue and create the conditions for productive debate. This involves helping teams clarify what's at stake, weigh alternatives, and commit to a course of action. It also requires defining the decision at hand, exploring trade-offs, and considering how people will justify their choice, building both confidence and accountability.

The Payoff

By embedding these questions into team routines, leaders can shift their culture from hesitation to action—enabling faster, smarter decisions and more empowered teams.

dialogues—through which assumptions are challenged or go unchallenged, information is shared or not shared, disagreements are brought to the surface or papered over. Dialogue is the basic unit of work in an organization. The quality of the dialogue determines how people gather and process information, how they make decisions, and how they feel about one another and about the outcome of these decisions. Dialogue can lead to new ideas and speed as a competitive advantage. It is the single-most important factor underlying the productivity and growth of the knowledge worker. Indeed, the tone and content of dialogue shapes people's behaviors and beliefs—that is, the corporate culture—faster and more permanently than any reward system, structural change, or vision statement I've seen.

Breaking a culture of indecision requires a leader who can engender intellectual honesty and trust in the connections between people. By using each encounter with his or her employees as an opportunity to model open, honest, and decisive dialogue, the leader sets the tone for the entire organization.

But setting the tone is only the first step. To transform a culture of indecision, leaders must also see to it that the organization's "social operating mechanisms"—that is, the executive committee meetings, budget and strategy reviews, and other situations through which the people of a corporation do business—have honest dialogue at their center. These mechanisms set the stage. Tightly linked and consistently practiced, they establish clear lines of accountability for reaching decisions and executing them.

Follow-through and feedback are the final steps in creating a decisive culture. Successful leaders use follow-through and honest feedback to reward high achievers, coach those who are struggling, and redirect the behaviors of those blocking the organization's progress.

In sum, leaders can create a culture of decisive behavior through attention to their own dialogue, the careful design of social operating mechanisms, and appropriate follow-through and feedback.

It All Begins with Dialogue

Studies of successful companies often focus on their products, business models, or operational strengths: Microsoft's world-conquering Windows operating system, Dell's mass customization, Walmart's logistical prowess. Yet products and operational strengths aren't what really set the most successful organizations apart—they can all be rented or imitated. What can't be easily duplicated are the decisive dialogues and robust operating mechanisms and their links to feedback and follow-through. These factors constitute an organization's most enduring competitive advantage, and they are heavily dependent on the character of dialogue that a leader exhibits and thereby influences throughout the organization.

Decisive dialogue is easier to recognize than to define. It encourages incisiveness and creativity and brings coherence to seemingly fragmented and unrelated ideas. It allows tensions to surface and then resolves them by fully airing every relevant viewpoint. Because such dialogue is a process of intellectual inquiry rather than of advocacy, a search for truth rather than a contest, people feel emotionally committed to the outcome. The outcome seems "right" because people have helped shape it. They are energized and ready to act.

Not long ago, I observed the power of a leader's dialogue to shape a company's culture. The setting was the headquarters of a major U.S. multinational. The head of one of the company's largest business units was making a strategy presentation to the CEO and a few of his senior lieutenants. Sounding confident, almost cocky, the unit head laid out his strategy for taking his division from number three in Europe to number one. It was an ambitious plan that hinged on making rapid, sizable market-share gains in Germany, where the company's main competitor was locally based and four times his division's size. The CEO commended his unit head for the inspiring and visionary presentation, then initiated a dialogue to test whether the plan was realistic. "Just how are you going to make these gains?" he wondered aloud. "What other alternatives have you considered? What customers do you plan to acquire?" The unit manager hadn't thought that far ahead. "How have you defined the customers' needs in new and unique ways? How many salespeople do you have?" the CEO asked.

"Ten," answered the unit head.

"How many does your main competitor have?"

"Two hundred," came the sheepish reply.

The boss continued to press: "Who runs Germany for us? Wasn't he in another division up until about three months ago?"

Had the exchange stopped there, the CEO would have only humiliated and discouraged this unit head and sent a message to others in attendance that the risks of thinking big were unacceptably high. But the CEO wasn't interested in killing the strategy and demoralizing the business unit team. Coaching through questioning, he wanted to inject some realism into the dialogue. Speaking bluntly, but not angrily or unkindly, he told the unit manager that he would need more than bravado to take on a formidable German competitor on its home turf. Instead of making a frontal assault, the CEO suggested, why not look for the competition's weak spots and win on speed of execution? Where are the gaps in your competitor's product line? Can you innovate something that can fill those gaps? What customers are the most likely buyers of such a product? Why not zero in on them? Instead of aiming for overall market-share gains, try resegmenting the market. Suddenly, what had appeared to be a dead end opened into new insights, and by the end of the meeting, it was decided that the manager would rethink the strategy and return in 90 days with a more realistic alternative. A key player whose strategy proposal had been flatly rejected left the room feeling energized, challenged, and more sharply focused on the task at hand.

Think about what happened here. Although it might not have been obvious at first, the CEO was not trying to assert his authority or diminish the executive. He simply wanted to ensure that the competitive realities were not glossed over and to coach those in attendance on both business acumen and organizational capability as well as on the fine art of asking the right questions. He was challenging the proposed strategy not for personal reasons but for business reasons.

The dialogue affected people's attitudes and behavior in subtle and not so subtle ways: They walked away knowing that they should look for opportunities in unconventional ways and be prepared to answer the inevitable tough questions. They also knew that the CEO was on their side. They became more convinced that growth was possible and that action was necessary. And something else happened: They began to adopt the CEO's tone in subsequent meetings. When, for example, the head of the German unit met with his senior staff to brief them on the new approach to the German market, the questions he fired at his sales chief and product development head were pointed, precise, and aimed directly at putting the new strategy into action. He had picked up on his boss's style of relating to others as well as his way of eliciting, sifting, and analyzing information. The entire unit grew more determined and energized.

The chief executive didn't leave the matter there, though. He followed up with a one-page, handwritten letter to the unit head stating the essence of the dialogue and the actions to be executed. And in 90 days, they met again to discuss the revised strategy. (For more on fostering decisive dialogue, see the sidebar "Dialogue Killers.")

Dialogue Killers

Is the dialogue in your meetings an energy drain? If it doesn't energize people and focus their work, watch for the following:

Dangling Dialogue

Symptom:

Confusion prevails. The meeting ends without a clear next step. People create their own self-serving interpretations of the meeting, and no one can be held accountable later when goals aren't met.

Remedy:

Give the meeting closure by ensuring that everyone knows who will do what, by when. Do it in writing if necessary, and be specific.

Information Clogs

Symptom:

Failure to get all the relevant information into the open. An important fact or opinion comes to light after a decision has been reached, which reopens the decision. This pattern happens repeatedly.

Remedy:

Ensure that the right people are in attendance in the first place. When missing information is discovered, disseminate it immediately. Make the expectation for openness and candor explicit by asking, "What's missing?" Use coaching and sanctions to correct information hoarding.

Piecemeal Perspectives

Symptom:

People stick to narrow views and self-interests and fail to acknowledge that others have valid interests.

Remedy:

Draw people out until you're sure all sides of the issue have been represented. Restate the common purpose repeatedly to keep everyone focused on the big picture. Generate alternatives. Use coaching to show people how their work contributes to the overall mission of the enterprise.

Free-for-All

Symptom:

By failing to direct the flow of the discussion, the leader allows negative behaviors to flourish. "Extortionists" hold the whole group for ransom until others see it their way; "sidetrackers" go off on tangents, recount history by saying "When I did this 10 years ago . . . ," or delve into unnecessary detail; "silent liars" do not express their true opinions, or they agree to things they have no intention of doing; and "dividers" create breaches within the group by seeking support for their viewpoint outside the social operating mechanism or have parallel discussions during the meeting.

Remedy:

The leader must exercise inner strength by repeatedly signaling which behaviors are acceptable and by sanctioning those who persist in negative behavior. If less severe sanctions fail, the leader must be willing to remove the offending player from the group.

How Dialogue Becomes Action

The setting in which dialogue occurs is as important as the dialogue itself. The social operating mechanisms of decisive corporate cultures feature behaviors marked by four characteristics: openness, candor, informality, and closure. Openness means that the outcome is not predetermined. There's an honest search for alternatives and new discoveries. Questions like "What are we missing?" draw people in and signal the leader's willingness to hear all sides. Leaders create an atmosphere of safety that permits spirited discussion, group learning, and trust.

Candor is slightly different. It's a willingness to speak the unspeakable, to expose unfulfilled commitments, to air the conflicts that undermine apparent consensus. Candor means that people express their real opinions, not what they think team players are supposed to say. Candor helps wipe out the silent lies and pocket vetoes that occur when people agree to things they have no intention of acting on. It prevents the kind of unnecessary rework and revisiting of decisions that saps productivity.

Formality suppresses candor; informality encourages it. When presentations and comments are stiff and prepackaged, they signal that the whole meeting has been carefully scripted and orchestrated. Informality has the opposite effect. It reduces defensiveness. People feel more comfortable asking questions and reacting honestly, and the spontaneity is energizing.

If informality loosens the atmosphere, closure imposes discipline. Closure means that at the end of the meeting, people know exactly what they are expected to do. Closure produces decisiveness by assigning accountability and deadlines to people in an open forum. It tests a leader's inner strength and intellectual resources. Lack of closure, coupled with a lack of sanctions, is the primary reason for a culture of indecision.

A robust social operating mechanism consistently includes these four characteristics. Such a mechanism has the right people participating in it, and it occurs with the right frequency.

When Dick Brown arrived at Electronic Data Systems (EDS) in early 1999, he resolved to create a culture that did more than pay lip service to the ideals of collaboration, openness, and decisiveness. He had a big job ahead of him. EDS was known for its bright, aggressive people, but employees had a reputation for competing against one another at least as often as they pulled together. The organization was marked by a culture of lone heroes. Individual operating units had little or no incentive for sharing information or cooperating with one another to win business. There were few sanctions for "lone" behaviors and for failure to meet performance goals. And indecision was rife. As one company veteran puts it, "Meetings, meetings, and more meetings. People couldn't make decisions, wouldn't make decisions. They didn't have to. No accountability." EDS was losing business. Revenue was flat, earnings were on the decline, and the price of the company's stock was down sharply.

A central tenet of Brown's management philosophy is that "leaders get the behavior they tolerate." Shortly after he arrived at EDS, he installed six social operating mechanisms within one year that signaled he would not put up with the old culture of rampant individualism and information hoarding. One mechanism was the "performance call," as it is known around the company. Once a month, the top 100 or so EDS executives worldwide take part in a conference call where the past month's numbers and critical activities are reviewed in detail. Transparency and simultaneous information are the rules; information hoarding is no longer possible. Everyone knows who is on target for the year, who is ahead of projections, and who is behind. Those who are behind must explain the shortfall—and how they plan to get back on track. It's not enough for a manager to say she's assessing, reviewing, or analyzing a problem. Those aren't the words of someone who is acting, Brown says. Those are the words of someone getting ready to act. To use them in front of Brown is to invite two questions in response: When you've finished your analysis, what are you going to do? And how soon are you going to do it? The only way that Brown's people can answer those questions satisfactorily is to make a decision and execute it.

The performance calls are also a mechanism for airing and resolving the conflicts inevitable in a large organization, particularly when it comes to cross-selling in order to accelerate revenue growth. Two units may be pursuing the same customer, for example, or a customer serviced by one unit may be acquired by a customer serviced by another. Which unit should lead the pursuit? Which unit should service the merged entity? It's vitally important to resolve these questions. Letting them fester doesn't just drain emotional energy, it shrinks the organization's capacity to act decisively. Lack of speed becomes a competitive disadvantage.

Brown encourages people to bring these conflicts to the surface, both because he views them as a sign of organizational health and because they provide an opportunity to demonstrate the style of dialogue he advocates. He tries to create a safe environment for disagreement by reminding employees that the conflict isn't personal. Conflict in any global organization is built in. And, Brown believes, it's essential if everyone is going to think in terms of the entire organization, not just one little corner of it. Instead of seeking the solution favorable to their unit, they'll look for the solution that's best for EDS and its shareholders. It sounds simple, even obvious. But in an organization once characterized by lone heroes and self-interest, highly visible exercises in conflict resolution remind people to align their interests with the company as a whole. It's not enough to state the message once and assume it will sink in. Behavior is changed through repetition. Stressing the message over and over in social operating mechanisms like the monthly performance calls— and rewarding or sanctioning people based on their adherence to it—is one of Brown's most powerful tools for producing the behavioral changes that usher in genuine cultural change.

Of course, no leader can or should attend every meeting, resolve every conflict, or make every decision. But by designing social operating mechanisms that promote free-flowing yet productive dialogue, leaders strongly influence how others perform these tasks. Indeed, it is through these mechanisms that the work of shaping a decisive culture gets done.

Another corporation that employs social operating mechanisms to create a decisive culture is multinational pharmaceutical giant Pharmacia. The company's approach illustrates a point I stress repeatedly to my clients: structure divides; social operating mechanisms integrate. I hasten to add that structure is essential. If an organization didn't divide tasks, functions, and responsibilities, it would never get anything done. But social operating mechanisms are required to direct the various activities contained within a structure toward an objective. Well-designed mechanisms perform this integrating function. But no matter how well designed, the mechanisms also need decisive dialogue to work properly.

Two years after its 1995 merger with Upjohn, Pharmacia's CEO Fred Hassan set out to create an entirely new culture for the combined entity. The organization he envisioned would be collaborative, customer focused, and speedy. It would meld the disparate talents of a global enterprise to develop market-leading drugs—and do so faster than the competition. The primary mechanism for fostering collaboration: Leaders from several units and functions would engage in frequent, constructive dialogue.

The company's race to develop a new generation of antibiotics to treat drug-resistant infections afforded Pharmacia's management an opportunity to test the success of its culture-building efforts. Dr. Göran Endo, the chief of research and development, and Carrie Cox, the head of global business management, jointly created a social operating mechanism comprising some of the company's leading scientists, clinicians, and marketers. Just getting the three functions together regularly was a bold step. Typically, drug development proceeds by a series of handoffs. One group of scientists does the basic work of drug discovery, then hands off its results to a second group, which steers the drug through a year or more of clinical trials. If and when it receives the Food and Drug Administration's stamp of approval, it's handed off to the marketing people, who devise a marketing plan. Only then is the drug handed off to the sales department, which pitches it to doctors and hospitals. By supplanting this daisy-chain approach with one that made scientists, clinicians, and marketers jointly responsible for the entire flow of development and marketing, the two leaders aimed to develop a drug that better met the needs of patients, had higher revenue potential, and gained speed as a competitive advantage. And they wanted to create a template for future collaborative efforts.

The company's reward system reinforced this collaborative model by explicitly linking compensation to the actions of the group. Every member's compensation would be based on the time to bring the drug to market, the time for the drug to reach peak profitable share, and total sales. The system gave group members a strong incentive to talk openly with one another and to share information freely. But the creative spark was missing. The first few times the drug development group met, it focused almost exclusively on their differences, which were considerable. Without trafficking in clichés, it is safe to say that scientists, clinicians, and marketers tend to have different ways of speaking, thinking, and relating. And each tended to defend what it viewed as its interests rather than the interests of shareholders and customers. It was at this point that Endo and Cox took charge of the dialogue, reminding the group that it was important to play well with others but, even more important, to produce a drug that met patients' needs and to beat the competition.

Acting together, the two leaders channeled conversation into productive dialogue focused on a common task. They shared what they knew about developing and marketing pharmaceuticals and demonstrated how scientists could learn to think a little like marketers, and marketers a little like scientists. They tackled the emotional challenge of resolving conflicts in the open in order to demonstrate how to disagree, sometimes strongly, without animosity and without losing sight of their common purpose.

Indeed, consider how one dialogue helped the group make a decision that turned a promising drug into a success story. To simplify the research and testing process, the group's scientists had begun to search for an antibiotic that would be effective against a limited number of infections and would be used only as "salvage therapy" in acute cases, when conventional antibiotic therapies had failed. But intensive dialogue with the marketers yielded the information that doctors were receptive to a drug that would work against a wide spectrum of infections. They wanted a drug that could treat acute infections completely by starting treatment earlier in the course of the disease, either in large doses through an intravenous drip or in smaller doses with a pill. The scientists shifted their focus, and the result was Zyvox, one of the major pharmaceutical success stories of recent years. It has become the poster drug in Pharmacia's campaign for a culture characterized by cross-functional collaboration and speedy execution. Through dialogue, the group created a product that neither the scientists, clinicians, nor marketers acting by themselves could have envisioned or executed. And the mechanism that created this open dialogue is now standard practice at Pharmacia.

Follow-Through and Feedback

Follow-through is in the DNA of decisive cultures and takes place either in person, on the telephone, or in the routine conduct of a social operating mechanism. Lack of follow-through destroys the discipline of execution and encourages indecision.

A culture of indecision changes when groups of people are compelled to always be direct. And few mechanisms encourage directness more effectively than performance and compensation reviews, especially if they are explicitly linked to social operating mechanisms. Yet all too often, the performance review process is as ritualized and empty as the business meeting I described at the beginning of this article. Both the employee and his manager want to get the thing over with as quickly as possible. Check the appropriate box, keep up the good work, here's your raise, and let's be sure to do this again next year. Sorry—gotta run. There's no genuine conversation, no feedback, and worst of all, no chance for the employee to learn the sometimes painful truths that will help her grow and develop. Great compensation systems die for lack of candid dialogue and leaders' emotional fortitude.

At EDS, Dick Brown has devised an evaluation and review process that virtually forces managers to engage in candid dialogue with their subordinates. Everyone at the company is ranked in quintiles and rewarded according to how well they perform compared with their peers. It has proved to be one of the most controversial features of Dick Brown's leadership—some employees view it as a Darwinian means of dividing winners from losers and pitting colleagues against one another.

That isn't the objective of the ranking system, Brown insists. He views the ranking process as the most effective way to reward the company's best performers and show laggards where they need to improve. But the system needs the right sort of dialogue to make it work as intended and serve its purpose of growing the talent pool. Leaders must give honest feedback to their direct reports, especially to those who find themselves at the bottom of the rankings.

Brown recalls one encounter he had shortly after the first set of rankings was issued. An employee who had considered himself one of EDS's best performers was shocked to find himself closer to the bottom of the roster than the top. "How could this be?" the employee asked. "I performed as well this year as I did last year, and last year my boss gave me a stellar review." Brown replied that he could think of two possible explanations. The first was that the employee wasn't as good at his job as he thought he was. The second possibility was that even if the employee was doing as good a job as he did the previous year, his peers were doing better. "If you're staying the same," Brown concluded, "you're falling behind."

That exchange revealed the possibility—the likelihood, even—that the employee's immediate superior had given him a less-than-honest review the year before rather than tackle the unpleasant task of telling him where he was coming up short. Brown understands why a manager might be tempted to duck such a painful conversation. Delivering negative feedback tests

GE's Secret Weapon

Known for its state-of-the-art management practices, General Electric has forged a system of 10 tightly linked social operating mechanisms. Vital to GE's success, these mechanisms set goals and priorities for the whole company as well as for its individual business units and track each unit's progress toward those goals. CEO Jack Welch also uses the system to evaluate senior managers within each unit and reward or sanction them according to their performance.

Three of the most widely imitated of these mechanisms are the Corporate Executive Council (CEC), which meets four times a year; the annual leadership and organizational reviews, known as Session C; and the annual strategy reviews, known as S-1 and S-2. Most large organizations have similar mechanisms. GE's, however, are notable for their intensity and duration; tight links to one another; follow-through; and uninhibited candor, closure, and decisiveness.

At the CEC, the company's senior leaders gather for two-and-a-half days of intensive collaboration and information exchange. As these leaders share best practices, assess the external business environment, and identify the company's most promising opportunities and most pressing problems, Welch has a chance to coach managers and observe their styles of working, thinking, and collaborating. Among the 10 initiatives to emerge from these meetings in the past 14 years are GE's six sigma quality-improvement drive and its companywide e-commerce effort. These sessions aren't for the fainthearted—at times, the debates can resemble verbal combat. But by the time the CEC breaks up, everyone in attendance knows both what the corporate priorities are and what's expected of him or her.

At Session C meetings, Welch and GE's senior vice president for human resources, Bill Conaty, meet with the head of each business unit as well as his or her top HR executive to discuss leadership and organizational issues. In these intense 12- to 14-hour sessions, the attendees review the unit's prospective talent pool and its organizational priorities. Who needs to be promoted, rewarded, and developed? How? Who isn't making the grade? Candor is mandatory, and so is execution. The dialogue goes back and forth and links with the strategy of the business unit. Welch follows up each session with a handwritten note reviewing the substance of the dialogue and action items. Through this mechanism, picking and evaluating people has become a core competence at GE. No wonder GE is known as "CEO University."

The unit head's progress in implementing that action plan is among the items on the agenda at the S-1 meeting, held about two months after Session C. Welch, his chief financial officer, and members of the office of the CEO meet individually with each unit head and his or her team to discuss strategy for the next three years. The strategy, which must incorporate the companywide themes and initiatives that emerged from the CEC meetings, is subjected to intensive scrutiny and reality testing by Welch and the senior staff. The dialogue in the sessions is informal, open, decisive, and full of valuable coaching from Welch on both business and human resources issues. As in Session C, the dialogue about strategy links with people and organizational issues. Again, Welch follows up with a handwritten note in which he sets out what he expects of the unit head as a result of the dialogue.

S-2 meetings, normally held in November, follow a similar agenda to the S-1 meeting, except that they are focused on a shorter time horizon, usually 12 to 15 months. Here, operational priorities and resource allocations are linked.

Taken together, the meetings link feedback, decision making, and assessment of the organization's capabilities and key people. The mechanism explicitly ties the goals and performance of each unit to the overall strategy of the corporation and places a premium on the development of the next generation of leaders. The process is unrelenting in its demand for managerial accountability. At the same time, Welch takes the opportunity to engage in follow-through and feedback that is candid, on point, and focused on decisiveness and execution. This operating system may be GE's most enduring competitive advantage.

the strength of a leader. But critical feedback is part of what Brown calls "the heavy lifting of leadership." Avoiding it, he says, "sentences the organization to mediocrity." What's more, by failing to provide honest feedback, leaders cheat their people by depriving them of the information they need to improve.

Feedback should be many things—candid; constructive; relentlessly focused on behavioral performance, accountability, and execution. One thing it shouldn't be is surprising. "A leader should be constructing his appraisal all year long," Brown says, "and giving his appraisal all year long. You have 20, 30, 60 opportunities a year to share your observations. Don't let those opportunities pass. If, at the end of the year, someone is truly surprised by what you have to say, that's a failure of leadership."

. . .

Ultimately, changing a culture of indecision is a matter of leadership. It's a matter of asking hard questions: How robust and effective are our social operating mechanisms? How well are they linked? Do they have the right people and the right frequency? Do they have a rhythm and operate consistently? Is follow-through built in? Are rewards and sanctions linked to the outcomes of the decisive dialogue? Most important, how productive is the dialogue within these mechanisms? Is our dialogue marked by openness, candor, informality, and closure?

Transforming a culture of indecision is an enormous and demanding task. It takes all the listening skills, business acumen, and operational experience that a corporate leader can summon. But just as important, the job demands emotional fortitude, follow-through, and inner strength. Asking the right questions, identifying and resolving conflicts, providing candid, constructive feedback, and differentiating people with sanctions and rewards is never easy. Frequently, it's downright unpleasant. No wonder many senior executives avoid the task. In the short term, they spare themselves considerable emotional wear and tear. But their evasion sets the tone for an organization that can't share intelligence, make decisions, or face conflicts, much less resolve them. Those who evade miss the very point of effective leadership. Leaders with the strength to insist on honest dialogue and follow-through will be rewarded not only with a decisive organization but also with a workforce that is energized, empowered, and engaged.

Originally published in April 2001. Reprint R0601J

Drive Innovation with Better Decision-Making

by Linda A. Hill, Emily Tedards, and Taran Swan

To stay competitive, today's business leaders are investing millions in digital tools, agile methodologies, and lean strategies.

Too often, however, those efforts produce neither the breakthrough operational processes nor the blockbuster business models companies need—at least not before their competitors introduce their own advances. And a key culprit is the inability to make quick and effective innovation decisions.

The discovery-driven innovation processes companies now rely on involve an unprecedented number of choices, from big go/no-go gates that govern which ideas are pursued to countless decisions about how to conduct experiments, what data to collect, how to interpret findings, and how to act on them. But in companies that are just learning to experiment, too many decisions are made inefficiently or informed by past experience and narrow perspectives. As a result, critical risks aren't identified, and bad ideas hang around forever, eating up scarce resources and crushing the chances of bigger, more-transformative bets.

Take Pfizer. (One of us, Hill, has been a paid adviser to the company over the years.) In 2015 the pharmaceutical giant kicked off a digital transformation effort in its Global Clinical Supply (GCS) arm, which delivers more than a million doses of investigative medicines to thousands of clinical sites in over 70 countries each year. Doing so while maintaining clinical trial integrity is a complex task. Any issue, such as inadequate refrigeration, unclear instructions for medical professionals, or patients' failure to comply with regimens, could delay the development of potentially lifesaving treatments. By 2018, GCS had made significant progress with its digital initiatives. But with new medical and digital technologies on the horizon, Pfizer's strategy changed to focus exclusively on breakthrough drugs and vaccines. GCS needed to become ever more agile, innovative, and patient focused so that it could adapt to myriad clinical-site and patient needs. Findings from a cultural survey, however, underscored that the organization was struggling to make good, timely decisions about systems, processes, and capability innovations.

So GCS altered its approach on a number of fronts, creating cross-functional teams that were responsible for key decisions, changing the frequency of decision-making meetings, and improving team members' ability to robustly debate ideas. Those efforts paid off when Covid hit: Thanks in no small part to the quick-footed support of GCS, the first emergency authorization of the Pfizer-BioNTech vaccine was granted only 266 days after the declaration of the pandemic. (GCS's journey in advance

Idea in Brief

The Problem

Despite their embrace of agile and lean methodologies, many organizations looking to become more innovative are still struggling to move quickly on new ideas. That's often because of their outdated, inefficient approach to decision-making.

The Research

Over the past two decades the authors have worked with innovative companies across the globe, most recently focusing on incumbent firms that were transforming themselves into nimbler businesses, to learn what key challenges they faced and how they addressed them.

The Solution

Businesses need to strengthen and speed up their creative decision-making processes by including diverse perspectives, clarifying decision rights, matching the cadence of decisions to the pace of learning, and encouraging candid, robust conflict in service of a better experience for the end customer. Only then will all that rapid experimentation pay off.

of the pandemic will be described throughout this article; for more on the race to make the vaccine, see "The CEO of Pfizer on Developing a Vaccine in Record Time," HBR, May–June 2021.) GCS's success at rapidly delivering tens of thousands of doses of the vaccine candidates and collaborating with colleagues across Pfizer to develop solutions to the thorny challenge of preserving them at subzero temperatures is just the most prominent of its many recent innovation achievements, which range from real-time tracking of trial-drug shipments to personalized tests for cutting-edge therapies.

We've spent almost two decades studying leaders at highly innovative organizations and, more recently, incumbent firms that are on their way to becoming innovation powerhouses. When we looked closely at 65 of the companies that were on the journey to becoming more nimble, we found that the more successful ones were applying many agile and lean principles to decision-making itself. In this article we'll show what that means: including diverse perspectives, clarifying decision rights, matching the cadence of decision-making to the pace of learning, and encouraging candid, healthy conflict in service of a better experience for the end customer.

Diverse Perspectives

Research has long shown that diverse teams are better at identifying opportunities and risks in any problem-solving situation. But in organizations that are learning to experiment, four perspectives tend to be underrepresented in decision-making:

The customer perspective

It's hardly a surprise that the customer needs to be at the heart of all decisions, whether they're about new products, business models, or internal processes. But we find that customer intimacy is all too rare. Because of that, firms end up chasing problems that don't really matter to customers and miss opportunities to address their unarticulated pain points and desires.

The solution here is to include in your decision-making processes the people who are most closely connected with end customers: frontline operations staff, customer service employees, salespeople, and the customers themselves. Organizations that are good at this also tend to work closely with user experience or user interface teams, ethnographic researchers, or experts in human-centric design. And if you're developing a new business process or a digital tool for employees, remember that *their* voices need to be heard—in this case they are the customers who will use it.

To represent the voices of patients in clinical trials and the health care professionals working directly with them, Pfizer's GCS unit created a new function, Clinical Research Pharmacy, and recruited pharmacists (who had prior experience administering the treatments) to join it. Over time, the CRP came to play an integral role in decision-making at GCS. Its pharmacists' insights have led to innovations ranging from user-friendly package designs to virtual-reality training for health care providers.

The local perspective

Too often decisions in global companies are made at headquarters without adequately taking into account perspectives from different geographies. Yet people at headquarters rarely have the contextual intelligence required to judge which new business models, services, or operations are best suited to a local economy and regulatory environment. Getting local input can make a big difference.

At GCS, strategic decisions, even those that affected regional operations, had been made principally by U.S. teams. But once the unit began deliberately soliciting ideas from local managers, empowering them to innovate, it saw impressive improvements. For instance, when a new Latin America–based team was established, it used its expertise to cut the time it took to get trial medicines to local health care providers and patients from 55 to 20 days.

Even more prevalent is the failure to transfer local insights back to a business's core processes and products. Often small divisions in small markets can be quicker and more innovative than their larger counterparts in home markets. For example, eBay's successful Buy It Now button, which revolutionized e-commerce and helped shopping move online, was developed

How to Avoid Common Traps

A number of traditional decision-making habits can hinder agile decision-making. They need to be unlearned.

Don't let leaders and experts dominate

More often than not, at the end of decision-making processes, one individual confidently makes the final call. This frequently stems from something innocuous: a respect for expertise. The problem is, experts can quickly become naysayers who shut down conversation. That's dangerous since they're often the most wedded to the status quo. Imagine a team with one digital expert who dismisses others' ideas about technology as naive or infeasible. No one wants to look ill-informed, so team members are likely to keep silent.

To combat this, experts should be asked to provide evidence for their points of view just like everyone else, keeping the argument rooted in fact rather than opinion or politics. Some leaders remove themselves from the process once the problem has been framed, letting their teams make the ultimate choice. Leaders often tell us it can be hard to stay quiet; Jessie Woolley-Wilson, the CEO of the ed-tech company DreamBox Learning, admits, "I am the worst practitioner of that because I get so excited and want to bring energy to the discussion." But she reminds herself, "My goal is to make fewer and fewer decisions."

Don't let people go along to get along

Compromise to avoid conflict can be superficial—everyone agrees while in the room but disagrees after leaving it—and it usually prioritizes employees' needs over customer experience. A good way to avoid this problem is to have proponents of each alternative make the case for other options. That helps all involved broaden their points of view, empathize with the logic of their teammates, and make sure they really understand an idea before discarding it. People should be encouraged to ask questions like "What am I not seeing?" and "Where is my expertise creating blind spots?" and open-ended "what-if" questions to help them let go of any assumptions constraining their thinking.

Avoiding compromise can lead to novel solutions. In one company we studied, the marketing and product divisions were deadlocked over a new service that the product team envisioned offering through the company's mobile app. The marketing division believed it wouldn't bring in a large-enough return to justify the costs of adding it to the app. The service went nowhere for nearly three years, until the company brought in a new innovation leader who asked, "What if we promoted the service somewhere other than the app?" The ultimate solution this prompted was neither a compromise nor one of the two original options: The team developed the service and touted it over SMS and email. Ultimately, its success provided the data the marketing team needed to confidently add the feature to the mobile app.

Don't let people make a decision prematurely

Decision-makers trying to keep up with the pace of change typically lean toward urgency. But even in an agile framework, the leader's role is to sense when more learning or synthesis of ideas is necessary and encourage patience.

At P&G, when a team wants to scale up a new product idea, its executive sponsor requires evidence that the product offers an "irresistibly superior experience" to customers. If the results look promising but not compelling enough to support a launch, teams are encouraged to continue to incubate the idea. Running additional experiments and collecting more data often leads to pivots that increase the value proposition.

by eBay Germany and was based on its deep relationships with its user communities.

The data-informed perspective

Especially in years like the past one, when the business environment was in constant flux, relying on past experience to guide innovation efforts may lead a company astray. Lean methods call for testing ideas and using near-real-time quantitative and qualitative data to decide next steps. The challenge lies in making that information accessible to every decision-maker.

Data visualization provides a solution: It can allow timely, complex information to be interpreted by people from a variety of functional backgrounds, leveling the playing field so that those who are less data savvy can fully engage when making decisions.

At GCS, a new digital-business-operations group created visual dashboards that superimposed information about events such as weather, flight, and shipping route disruptions over supply chain data to predict risks to operations in real time. These dashboards, which were accessible to all team members, proved invaluable at the daily "light speed" meetings held to respond to the Covid crisis as it upended supply chains, shut down borders, and overwhelmed the hospitals running Pfizer's clinical trials. GCS teams were able to make critical decisions about the processes for supplying ongoing trials across the globe, including those for the new Covid vaccine candidates and antivirals. Despite the logistical challenges brought on by the pandemic and natural disasters from wildfires to hurricanes, the organization didn't miss a single delivery to trial patients.

The outside perspective

Even the best-intentioned innovators can get mired in their companies' dominant logic. Leaders of incumbent firms, especially ones that are still growing, albeit slowly, tend to reject bold ideas—ideas that present high risk as well as high reward, require new resources or capabilities, or threaten to cannibalize the core business. An outside view can help organizations contemplate those moves more seriously.

That outside view can come from within the company, however. GCS invited high-potential talent from other parts of Pfizer to join its leadership team permanently, increasing the group from six to 16 members. Many leaders at other firms ask less experienced, recently hired employees to attend C-suite meetings. Because these people aren't steeped in the company's inner workings, they ask questions that challenge core assumptions and help reframe strategic choices.

An outside perspective can also come from beyond the company's walls or even its industry. GCS, for example, invited people from Delta Air Lines' innovation lab to participate in a design workshop on the clinical trial experience for patients. Delta's boarding-pass scanner and bag-tracking capabilities sparked ideas for new ways that GCS could enhance its own shipment-tracking capabilities, ensuring that more patients got the right dose of the right drug at the right time.

Clear Decision Rights

As they recognize the need to bring together many points of view, a lot of organizations are relying more on decentralized networks of cross-functional teams, both permanent and ad hoc, to increase their agility. But this can have a downside: Involving more voices in a decision can mean less clarity about who ultimately owns it, slowing the innovation process and often prompting frustration and disengagement.

For example, when executives at a financial services firm asked their high-potential team leaders to identify and pursue new business models, the results were disappointing. The team leaders didn't understand that they'd been given the authority to make decisions themselves and often came back to the executives and suggested options to choose from, rather than proposing an intended plan of action. The team leaders also had a mixed experience. At first they were honored and energized by being selected for an innovative project. But later they became discouraged by the disconnect between their recommendations and the decisions of the executives—who'd fallen back into their habit of calling the shots—and ultimately, by the ambiguity about decision-making rights.

To effectively empower decision-makers, leaders must be explicit in every case about who will be *responsible* for executing the decision, who will be *accountable* for making it, who will be *consulted,* and who will be *informed.* (Creating and sharing a traditional RACI chart can do the trick here.) If leaders are delegating decisions to a group, they should specify the process to be used and the parameters of the group's authority for everyone involved.

GCS transferred ownership of the investigative drug supply from a single leader to cross-functional teams of four known as "tetrads." Each tetrad became responsible for one therapeutic area. The members were collectively accountable for decisions, and they had clear guidelines about when they should escalate a decision to the tetrad's executive sponsors. It took some months for everyone involved to feel confident about the new structure and to refine the guidelines, but ultimately the tetrads helped GCS kill less promising ideas faster, without having to push those choices up to senior leadership. With their enterprisewide view, the teams were also able to begin proposing more-innovative ideas for optimizing the whole clinical supply chain, such as how to pioneer delivery of highly personalized gene-therapy drugs.

The Right Cadence

Established companies tend to make innovation decisions on a fixed schedule, through quarterly or annual reviews at which senior teams step back, assess past plans, and make new ones. But in agile companies, innovation is based on discovery-driven learning. With each experiment, data and insights emerge that should be taken into consideration in setting up the next one. Leaders must encourage decisions to be made at a pace aligned with the learning cycle.

To gauge the right cadence for your meetings, think about how long it will take to gather enough data to validate (or disprove) your hypotheses. If you're learning quickly or confronting rapid change, you may need to make decisions more frequently. During the pandemic, for example, most leadership teams at companies we observed naturally increased the cadence of meetings. Given the unfolding nature of the crisis, every decision had to be considered a "working hypothesis," so they opted for short sessions daily over longer ones every few weeks. Many told us they hope to stick with the new, faster rhythm even after the pandemic is over.

The many decisions that come up daily in experimentation often call for continuous processes. For example, in one Indian organization we studied, the design team created a WhatsApp forum to collect rapid feedback on its proposals from the whole organization, including remote employees working closely with end users in the field. Because the channel was always available, designers could spontaneously solicit feedback from employees and apply it to decisions immediately.

But longer timelines can still be needed to create the space necessary for collaboration and information gathering, especially if you're contemplating big bets. When Kathy Fish, P&G's former chief research, development, and innovation officer, introduced the lean startup model to her organization, the business units supplemented their annual planning processes with a review of innovation portfolios every 90 days in order to issue metered funding to the initiatives in them. That gave teams enough time to conduct experiments and consolidate findings while preserving their momentum.

Good Fights

Inviting diverse sets of participants to well-timed decision-making forums doesn't automatically lead to the thorough vetting of ideas. This is where so many organizations get stuck: They fail to create a competitive marketplace of ideas, where genuine debate increases the odds that risks are identified and the most-promising projects are pursued.

In some dysfunctional teams, productive discourse is stymied by political infighting, defensive behavior, or hidden agendas. Critiques of ideas often become critiques of personalities, and employees don't trust that their ideas will be taken seriously. Often any real conversations and decisions happen "outside the room," so members of the group feel disenfranchised even though they've been asked to participate.

Yet an even more common cause of unproductive debate is a culture of politeness. Many people try to minimize differences as opposed to amplifying them, in an effort to avoid conflict. The effect is that those with minority views don't speak up or compromise too quickly when they're challenged. As a result bosses or experts tend to dominate the decision-making process no matter how diverse the assembled group is.

In both kinds of situations, leaders must stop worrying about whether people can collaborate and instead worry about whether they know how to argue. Leaders can encourage the psychological safety that promotes good fights in three ways:

Ask questions

Leaders need to avoid shutting down the conversation with solutions from the outset. Instead, they should be transparent about what they don't know. At P&G (which has also hired Hill as an adviser in the past), leaders are encouraged to ask these four questions in response to every experiment: *What did you learn? How do you know? What do you need to learn next? How can I help?* By demonstrating that they don't have all the answers, leaders help set the expectation that all present should share their opinions and that anyone can be wrong. They also create an environment in which people feel more comfortable challenging one another.

At Pfizer, team members were initially reluctant to disagree with vice president Michael Ku when he became the head of GCS. But as he learned to admit what he didn't know and adopted the habit of being the last person to share his thoughts in meetings, they became more comfortable speaking up.

Focus on the data

Data can provide a solid foundation for productive debate. Team members who have the same data visualizations in front of them are likelier to develop a shared understanding of problems— common ground on which they can add their unique perspectives. Ku ensured that all decisions made at GCS's monthly operational review were informed by data. When things had to move quickly during Covid, this kept the team from making

Why focus on decision-making?

In our almost 20 years of research with organizations across the globe, we have identified the most important factors that support innovation—whether it's the invention of new product or service offerings, business processes or models, or ways of organizing or cutting costs. They include both cultural factors and capabilities.

All firms

Creative abrasion	**Creative agility**	**Creative resolution**	**Additional factors**
is the ability to generate a marketplace of ideas through discourse and debate.	is the ability to do discovery-driven learning.	is the ability to make decisions that combine disparate and sometimes even opposing ideas.	include decision-making basics, customer intimacy, and innovation investment.

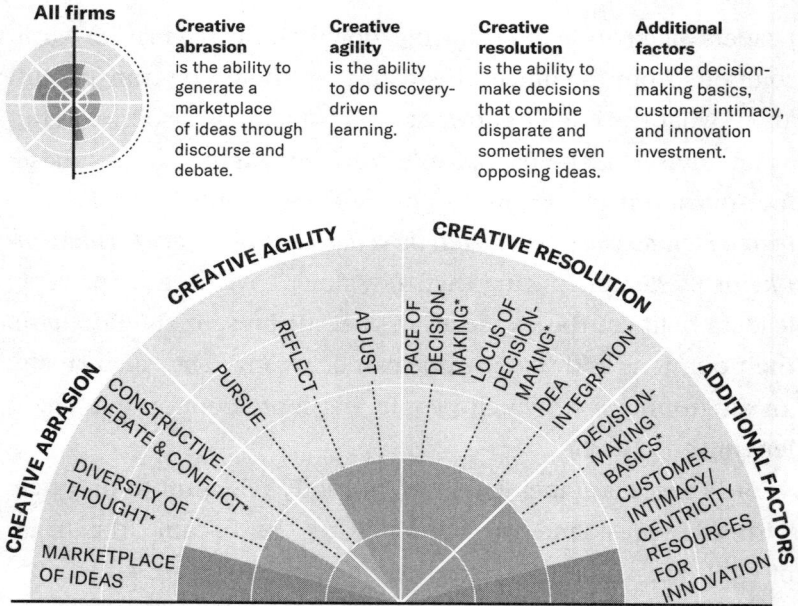

CREATIVE AGILITY

CREATIVE RESOLUTION

CREATIVE ABRASION

ADDITIONAL FACTORS

REFLECT

PURSUE

CONSTRUCTIVE DEBATE & CONFLICT*

DIVERSITY OF THOUGHT*

MARKETPLACE OF IDEAS

ADJUST

PACE OF DECISION-MAKING*

LOCUS OF DECISION-MAKING*

IDEA INTEGRATION*

DECISION-MAKING BASICS*

CUSTOMER INTIMACY/ CENTRICITY

RESOURCES FOR INNOVATION

*Decision-making capabilities

choices based on emotion or past experiences that were no longer relevant.

Articulate a shared purpose

Aligning the whole organization around a common, meaningful purpose (why we exist and whom we serve) gives people permission to fight about new ideas, because they all agree about what

In more-recent research, we've found that companies trying to become more innovative tend to do better at the cultural factors but have weaker capabilities, including decision-making.

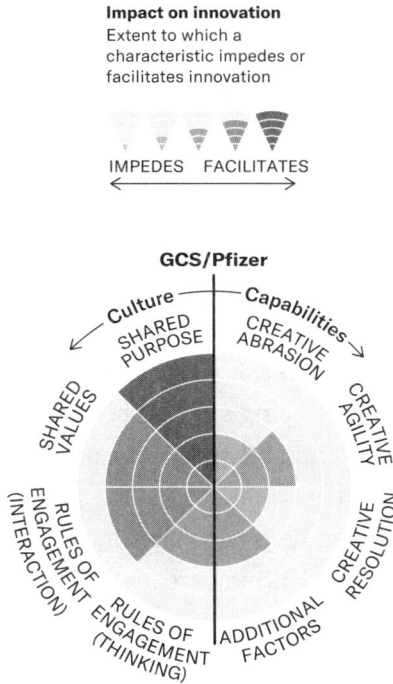

Impact on innovation
Extent to which a characteristic impedes or facilitates innovation

IMPEDES   FACILITATES

GCS/Pfizer

they're fighting for. Ideally the purpose will serve as a framework that ensures that decisions benefit the end user or customer.

A shared ambition can keep debates from getting personal. At one retail company we studied, a team created avatars for key customer segments. "Ali" was the avatar for urban Millennials, for instance. Whenever a discussion started to get more personal than substantive, someone would intervene and ask, "What does

Ali need from us all right now?" That encouraged the team to focus on a joint concern for customers instead of descending into a winner-takes-all argument.

A purpose can also encourage criticism rather than silent politeness. A real challenge in companies learning to be agile is killing "walking zombies"—projects without enough value to justify their continuation. To meet it, leaders should remind teams of their purpose. When Ku first took the reins at GCS, most people were reluctant to criticize others' ideas. Decision-makers interpreted silence as agreement that an idea was worth pursuing, so the number of projects underway became overwhelming. Ku's first priority was to align the entire team around a shared purpose: "Patients First." In debates about which initiatives to pursue, people learned to ask, "Is that the best solution for the patient?" rather than staying silent. The team soon found itself rejecting more ideas and able to focus more effort on those that enhanced the patient experience.

A common purpose helps decision-makers focus on solving problems rather than fulfilling personal agendas. In the midst of Covid, while everyone was working 24/7, Ku observed with pride that leaders in GCS were advocating for decisions that were in the best interests of the patient even when doing so meant more work for their own functional areas.

Leadership Matters

Organizations and teams must adopt new behaviors to make informed decisions more quickly, but managers need to change, too. Too many leaders act unilaterally, swooping in to save the day with the "right" answers—especially during a crisis. But when innovation is called for, leaders need to create environments in which their people can find answers on their own. It takes courage and practice to step back and let others make decisions and especially to avoid taking the bait when teams naturally try to delegate up the chain. But until you adopt this new way of working yourself, your organization will never be as innovative as it could be.

Originally published in November–December 2021. Reprint R2106D

Discussion Guide

Are you feeling inspired by what you've read in this collection? Do you want to share the ideas in the articles or explore the insights you've gleaned with others? This discussion guide offers an opportunity to dig a little deeper, with questions to prompt personal reflection and to start conversations with your team.

You don't need to have read the book from beginning to end to use this guide. Choose the questions that apply to the articles you have read or that you feel might spark the liveliest discussion.

Reflect on key takeaways from your reading to help you adopt the ideas and techniques you want to integrate into your work as a leader. What tools can you share with your team to help everyone be their best? Becoming the leader you want to be starts with a detailed plan—and a commitment to carrying it out.

1. Reflect on a time when you faced a difficult decision that had no clear, right answer. How did you approach it, and what factors did you weigh when deciding? What did you learn from the challenge of making the decision?

2. Chapter 2 discusses eight psychological traps that affect our decisions: anchoring, status-quo, sunk-cost, confirming evidence, framing, overconfidence, prudence, and recallability. When has one of these traps influenced an important decision of yours? How have you tried to prevent that trap from influencing you going forward?

3. When making decisions, how do you balance gut instinct with data? Are there types of decisions where going with your gut or being data-driven tends to work better for you? Why?

4. Have you ever faced a situation where your past experience made you overconfident or led you astray? What happened? What strategies have you used to challenge assumptions that are based on your past experience?

5. How does your decision-making differ in circumstances where you can't influence the outcome versus those where you can? What approach do you use for each situation, and why?

6. How do you try to reduce *noise* (chance variability caused by a random factor, such as someone's mood or the weather) to ensure consistency in your decisions? What tools, checklists, or frameworks do you find helpful? What else could you do to increase that consistency?

7. Have you found that human insight clearly outperformed AI-based recommendations in certain situations? What were they, and why do you think human judgment was more effective? In your experience with today's AI tools, are there rules of thumb for when relying on them can make decisions more—or less—effective?

8. Think of a time when you had to decide whether certain data was relevant to a decision you were facing. What aspects of the data made it hard to evaluate? What questions, habits, or practices helped you evaluate the data?

9. Can you recall a situation when having too little data slowed down your decision-making? What happened, and how did you move forward? What have you learned about making good decisions with less data than you'd like?

10. Chapter 7 names five decision roles: recommend, agree, perform, input, decide. When has ambiguity around these roles been a problem in your organization? What were the results? In your work, what steps could you take to help clarify who recommends, who decides, and who executes?

11. Think about the advisers you consult (formally or informally, inside and outside your organization) when making tough decisions. How varied are their perspectives and their advice? What could you do to broaden your idea network and ensure you're getting a range of viewpoints?

12. What strategies or methods does your team use to weigh options and courses of action? Has the team's typical process ever led to decisions that turned out badly? Why, and what did the group learn from these occasions?

13. Have you worked in a culture whose decisions were routinely delayed or avoided? What were the signs of indecision, and how did it affect your work or your team's performance? How did that culture compare with other cultures you've been a part of where decisions were made more quickly?

14. What decision-making bottlenecks or outdated processes or norms have held back innovation in the organizations you've worked for? Chapter 10 discusses four ways to align decision-making with agile approaches: having diverse points of view, clarifying decision rights, matching the

cadence of decisions to the pace of learning, and encouraging candid conflict. Which of these strategies could be improved in your organization, and how would you do it?

15. What other sources on decision-making have had a significant impact on your work? Were there voices or subtopics you missed in this collection? Were there voices or subtopics included that surprised you?

16. After reading and reflecting on this book and discussing it with people on your team, write down the ideas and techniques you want to try. Think of how you might experiment and implement them in both the short term and long term. Draft a plan to move forward.

Notes

Chapter 3: Fooled by Experience

1. Lars Lefgren, Brennan Platt, and Joseph Rice, "Sticking with What (Barely) Worked: A Test of Outcome Bias," *Management Science* 61, no. 5 (2014), https://doi.org/10.1287/mnsc.2014.1966.

2. Francesca Gino, Don A. Moore, and Max H. Bazerman, "No Harm, No Foul: The Outcome Bias in Ethical Judgments," Harvard Business School 2009, https://www.hbs.edu/ris/Publication Files/08-080_1751f2c7-abe2-402b-9959-1d8190ebf62a.pdf.

3. Jerker Denrell, "Vicarious Learning, Undersampling of Failure, and the Myths of Management," *Organization Science* 14, no. 3 (2003), http://pubsonline.informs.org/doi/abs/10.1287/orsc.14.2.227.15164.

4. Sun Hyun Park, James D. Westphal, and Ithai Stern, "Set Up for a Fall: The Insidious Effects of Flattery and Opinion Conformity Towards Corporate Leaders," *Administrative Science Quarterly* 56, no. 2 (2011), http://asq.sagepub.com/content/56/2/257.abstract.

About the Contributors

Joseph L. Badaracco is the John Shad Professor of Business Ethics at Harvard Business School, where he has taught courses on leadership, strategy, corporate responsibility, and management. His books on these subjects include the *New York Times* bestseller *Leading Quietly* (Harvard Business School Press, 2002), *Defining Moments* (Harvard Business School Press, 1997), *Step Back: How to Bring the Art of Reflection into Your Busy Life* (Harvard Business Review Press, 2020), and his latest book, *Your True Moral Compass.*

Tom Blaser is a data scientist and AI engineer at Augment Technologies.

Marcia W. Blenko is an advisory partner in Bain & Company's Boston office. She cofounded and formerly led Bain's Global Organization Practice. She is a coauthor of *Decide and Deliver: Five Steps to Breakthrough Performance in Your Organization* (Harvard Business Press, 2010).

Ram Charan serves on seven private and public boards across the globe and is the author or coauthor of 36 books and several HBR articles on corporate governance. He is a coauthor of *Boards That Lead: When to Take Charge, When to Partner, and When to Stay Out of the Way* (Harvard Business Review Press, 2013).

Amy C. Edmondson is the Novartis Professor of Leadership and Management at Harvard Business School. Her latest book is *Right Kind of Wrong: The Science of Failing Well.*

Linnea Gandhi is a doctoral student at the Wharton School at the University of Pennsylvania. Prior, she taught at the University of Chicago Booth School of Business and ran a behavioral science consulting firm.

John S. Hammond was a consultant on decision-making, a professor at Harvard Business School, and a coauthor of *Smart Choices: A Practical Guide to Making Better Decisions* (Harvard Business School Press, 1998).

Linda A. Hill is the Wallace Brett Donham Professor of Business Administration and the faculty chair of the Leadership Initiative at Harvard Business School. She is the author of *Becoming a Manager* (Harvard Business School Press, 1992), a coauthor of *Being the Boss* and *Collective Genius* (Harvard Business Review Press, 2011 and 2014, respectively), and a coauthor of *Genius at Scale: How Great Leaders Drive Innovation* (Harvard Business Review Press, 2026).

Robin M. Hogarth was a cognitive psychologist and a professor emeritus at Pompeu Fabra University, Barcelona. The past president of the Society for Judgment and Decision Making as well as of the European Association for Decision Making, he authored numerous scientific and professional papers and several books, including *The Myth of Experience*, with Emre Soyer, and *Educating Intuition*.

Adam Job is the senior director of the Strategy Lab at the Boston Consulting Group's BCG Henderson Institute.

Daniel Kahneman was the Eugene Higgins Professor Emeritus of Psychology and a professor emeritus of psychology and public affairs at Princeton University. He was awarded the Nobel Prize in Economic Sciences in 2002 for his work (with Amos Tversky) on cognitive biases.

Ralph L. Keeney is a professor emeritus at Duke University's Fuqua School of Business, a coauthor of *Smart Choices* (Harvard Business School Press, 1998), and the author of *Give Yourself a Nudge*.

Michael Luca is a professor of business administration and the director of the Technology and Society Initiative at Johns Hopkins University Carey Business School.

Tanya Menon is a professor of management and human resources at Ohio State University's Fisher College of Business. She is a coauthor of *Stop Spending, Start Managing: Strategies to Transform Wasteful Habits* (Harvard Business Review Press, 2016).

Mihnea Moldoveanu is the Marcel Desautels Professor of Integrative Thinking, a professor of economic analysis, the director of the Desautels Centre for Integrative Thinking, and the director of Rotman Digital at the Rotman School of Management at the University of Toronto. He is the author (with Das Narayandas) of *The Future of Executive Development* and *Soft Skills: How to See, Measure, and Build the Skills That Make Us Uniquely Human.*

Steven Morris is the author of the bestselling *The Beautiful Business* and the CEO of Matter Consulting, which helps leaders align culture, brand, and strategy to build enduring organizations. With experience advising over 3,300 leaders at companies like Google, Qualcomm, Coca-Cola, and Habitat for Humanity, he is recognized as a leading voice on whole-human leadership and business transformation.

Mark Mortensen is a professor of organizational behavior at INSEAD and, for over 20 years, has studied and consulted on collaboration and organization design, with a focus on hybrid, virtual, and globally distributed work. He publishes regularly in *Harvard Business Review, MIT Sloan Management Review,* and INSEAD Knowledge and is a regular fixture in popular press outlets like the BBC, the *Economist,* the *Financial Times,* and *Fortune.*

Alex "Sandy" Pentland is a Human-AI Fellow at Stanford University and the Toshiba Professor of Media Arts and Science with the Media Lab, Sloan School of Management, and College of Computing at the Massachusetts Institute of Technology. He is a member of the National Academy of Engineering, an adviser to the board of the Abu Dhabi Investment Authority Lab, and a former adviser to Google, AT&T, the UN secretary general, and several companies spun off from his research lab.

Howard Raiffa was the Frank Plumpton Ramsey Professor Emeritus of Managerial Economics at Harvard Business School and a coauthor of *Smart Choices* (Harvard Business School Press, 1998).

Martin Reeves is the chair of Boston Consulting Group's BCG Henderson Institute. He is a coauthor, with Jack Fuller, of *The Imagination Machine* (Harvard Business Review Press, 2021) and a coauthor, with Bob Goodson, of *Like: The Button That Changed the World* (Harvard Business Review Press, 2025).

Paul Rogers was formerly a partner in Bain & Company's London and Middle East offices. He cofounded and led Bain's Global Organization Practice. He is a coauthor of *Decide and Deliver* (Harvard Business Press, 2010).

Andrew M. Rosenfield is the CEO and managing partner of the consulting firm The Greatest Good Group.

Phil Rosenzweig is a professor emeritus at IMD in Switzerland, where he was a faculty member from 1996 to 2021. He is the author of several books and articles about decision-making, including *The Halo Effect . . . and the Eight Other Business Delusions That Deceive Managers*.

Emre Soyer is a behavioral scientist and the coauthor of *The Myth of Experience* with Robin M. Hogarth. He is the founder of SOYER Decision Advisory, which provides talks, workshops, and projects on critical thinking, decision-making, and negotiating to organizations worldwide. He is also an adjunct professor of decision-making and negotiations in business schools, including INSEAD and Bayes Business School.

Taran Swan is a managing partner at Paradox Strategies and a provider and creator of advisory services, experiences, and tools that enable organizations to navigate the paradoxes of leadership, innovation, and diversity.

Emily Tedards is a doctoral student in the Organizational Behavior unit at Harvard Business School and a fellow at Harvard Kennedy's Reimagining the Economy initiative. She is a coauthor of *Genius at Scale* (Harvard Business Review Press, 2026).

Leigh Thompson is the J. Jay Gerber Distinguished Professor of Dispute Resolution and Organizations at the Kellogg School of Management, Northwestern University. Her books include *Negotiating the Sweet Spot, Creative Conspiracy, Making the Team, The Mind and Heart of the Negotiator, The Truth about Negotiations,* and *Stop Spending, Start Managing.* Visit her website at leighthompson.com.

Melody Wilding is an executive coach, a human behavior professor, and the author of *Managing Up.* Download a free chapter at managingup.com/chapter/.

Index